After-School Meal Planner

Annabel Karmel's
After-School Meal Planner

EBURY
PRESS

First published in 2006

Text copyright © Annabel Karmel 2006
Photographs copyright © Dave King 2006

Annabel Karmel has asserted her right
to be identified as the author of this
work under the Copyright, Designs and
Patents Act 1988.

First published by Ebury Press
Random House, 20 Vauxhall Bridge
Road, London SW1V 2SA

Random House Australia (Pty) Limited
20 Alfred Street, Milsons Point, Sydney,
New South Wales 2061, Australia
Random House New Zealand Limited
18 Poland Road, Glenfield, Auckland
10, New Zealand

Random House South Africa (Pty)
Limited, Isle of Houghton, Corner
Boundary Road & Carse O'Gowrie,
Houghton 2198, South Africa

The Random House Group Limited Reg.
No. 954009

www.randomhouse.co.uk

A CIP catalogue record for this book is
available from the British Library

ISBN 0 09 19050 01

Editor: Helena Caldon
Designer: Lisa Pettibone
Photographer: Dave King
Stylist: Jo Harris
Home economist: Dagmar Vesely
Nutritionists: Seki Tijani and
  Fiona Hunter
Printed and bound in China by C&C Offset
Printing Co., Ltd.

**To my children,
Nicholas, Lara and
Scarlett.**

Contents

0 Introduction and meal planner 6

1 Savoury snacks, sweet treats 16

2 Pasta pronto 48

3 Fishy business 68

4 Time for chicken 86

5 Meaty goodness 106

6 We love our veg 126

7 What's for pud? 144

8 More cookies and cakes please! 164

Index 186

Introduction

When children come home from school they are usually starving, so this is a great opportunity to get them to eat something healthy. Unfortunately, most children tend to head straight for the crisps or biscuit tin when they get home, as these are the only things available to snack on.

These days a lot of children eat more between meals than they do at mealtimes, so it's important to spend a little time making sure there are some healthy snacks around. Keep the fruit bowl full; whilst whole fruit tends not to get eaten, if you were to spend a few minutes cutting up a selection of colourful fruits or threading fruits onto a skewer, it could make all the difference. If fruit isn't their thing, have a low shelf in the fridge where there is always a selection of healthy snacks for your children to help themselves to after school, such as raw vegetables and cherry tomatoes with a tasty dip, pitta pockets, wraps or pasta salads.

The aim of good nutrition is to supply the body with a variety of the vitamins and minerals needed for energy production, growth and repair. This is especially important during the rapid development years of childhood, puberty and adolescence. During these times of growth and change young people require a vast range of nutrients to build a strong immune system, to aid the development of the brain and bones and organs such as the lungs and heart.

Processed foods provide three-quarters of the saturated fat and salt that we eat, so the single most effective thing you can do to improve your child's diet is to cut back on these foods and prepare more meals yourself from fresh ingredients. It's easy to rely on convenience or snack foods to get by, but eating together as a family is important, even if you only do it a few times a week. Meals are not just about nutrition – they should be relaxed family occasions and are a good chance to catch up on what your child is up to.

By feeding your child a varied diet you should include the key nutrients required for growth and development; and because vitamins and minerals work in synergy, it's important to include all members of the team.

In this book I have put together a collection of tasty, quick and easy-to-prepare suppers and snacks which make use of all the important foods that children need to grow up healthy and strong.

The main building blocks of foods fall into three categories:

Carbohydrates

Wholemeal bread, wholemeal pasta, brown rice, oats, oatcakes, all fruits and vegetables.

The chief function of carbohydrates is to provide energy for the body and the brain, so they are important for growing children who have a greater need for energy than adults. A child's appetite may seem to swing from all to nothing, but this is not unusual and an increased appetite might just signal that they are entering a growth spurt.

It is important to include a wide range of wholegrains, such as rice and oats, pulses, wholemeal breads, and other healthy carbohydrates, such as fruits and vegetables, in our diets. These include complex carbohydrates which help satisfy the appetite for longer and provide the body with a more sustained release of energy.

Because these complex carbohydrates do not trigger blood sugar highs and lows, they can help to minimize mood swings, poor concentration and hyperactive episodes.

Although not classed as a nutrient, carbohydrates also provide essential fibre. Constipation can be a serious problem which can lead to digestive problems, sluggishness, poor immunity and erratic behaviour. Naturally fibre-rich foods help keep elimination regular and they also have a role to play in balancing blood sugar levels, as fibre slows the breakdown of carbohydrates into sugar.

Protein

Chicken, fish, meat, eggs, milk, cheese, yoghurt, nuts, seeds, pulses, lentils, quinoa (a South American grain), soya products: milk, yoghurt and tofu.

Our bodies are made up of approximately 25 per cent protein, because it is essential for building hair, skin, nails, bones, cartilage, ligaments and hormones – which work like chemical messengers between the glands, brain and nervous system. Although a growing child requires more protein than an adult, be aware that too much can over-burden the kidneys. Spread their protein intake throughout the day and ensure that at least one serving of protein is of animal origin. Red meat is a good source of protein, but it also provides the best and most easily absorbed source of iron – so try to encourage your child to eat red meat at least twice a week. Iron deficiency is the most common nutritional deficiency and affects about 15 per cent of young children. In addition, 46 per cent of girls aged 11 to 18 are deficient in iron and 93 per cent of females aged 16 to 18 are not meeting the recommended daily allowance of iron.

If you don't eat red meat, foods such as spinach, fortified breakfast cereals and dried apricots are also useful sources of iron. However, it is difficult for our bodies to absorb iron from a non-meat source unless you eat some vitamin C-rich foods in the same meal. So, to improve iron absorption include fruit, such as kiwis or berry fruits, or give a vitamin C-rich juice like orange or cranberry with meals.

Protein can also be found in dairy products, which have the additional nutritional advantage of providing the best and most easily absorbed source of calcium. Calcium is vital during childhood and teenage years to ensure the development of strong bones and teeth. Even during periods of slow growth children need two to four times more calcium per kilogram of body weight than adults. According to the National Dairy Council in Britain at least two and a half million young people and women do not include enough calcium in their diet.

Essential fatty acids

Oily fish (mackerel, salmon, sardines, tuna), eggs, nuts, seeds and avocado.

Choosing the right fats for your children is essential for the healthy development and functioning of the brain and nervous system, eyes, skin and hormone balance. Essential Fatty Acids (EFAs), such as Omega-3 and 6, cannot be produced by the body and therefore they must be obtained from food. As well as providing the building blocks and fuel for the brain, EFAs also help promote smooth skin and can alleviate dry, itchy skin conditions such as eczema. EFAs are especially important during teenage years when they work to balance hormone levels.

Oily fish such as salmon, mackerel, fresh tuna and sardines are rich in Omega-3 fatty acids, which are also believed to boost children's brain power. Research shows that brain function and memory may all be improved through an increase of these Omega-3 fatty acids, because they speed up the rate at which messages are sent around the brain. They also improve the speed and efficiency with which the eyes work.

Most children do not eat enough Omega-3 fats, so including oily fish in the diet can help to improve concentration in children who have attention deficit disorder and also help to improve the performance of children who are dyspraxic. If you have concerns about your child, consult your GP about having him or her tested for a deficiency in essential fatty acids.

Be aware that whilst fresh tuna is a good source of Omega-3 fatty acids, tinned tuna is not a good substitute because the EFAs are lost in the processing.

Water

Although not a nutrient, water is essential for keeping the cells in the body hydrated, for the processing of all chemical reactions, for keeping the digestive system regular and also for energy production. Water should always be the first option when offering a child a drink; however, sometimes that can prove to be a battle. Make sure that they are drinking plain water regularly throughout the day and dilute any fruit juices to reduce their sugar intake.

Salt

The liking for salt and salty foods is a learned taste preference and most children eat twice as much salt as they should. As I said earlier, approximately three-quarters of the salt we eat comes from processed foods such as packet and tinned soups, instant noodles, sausages and burgers, pizzas, chicken nuggets and salty snacks.

Some foods are now labelled with the salt content per serving while others may give the amount of sodium in grams per 100 g of food. If you want to know what the salt content is of the foods you are eating, you need to multiply the sodium figure by 2.5 and set it against the weight of the serving, i.e. 1 g of sodium per 100 g = 2.5 g salt. In general, foods that contain more than 0.5 g of sodium per 100 g are high in salt and are best avoided. Five grams of salt is equivalent to one level teaspoon.

A high salt intake is believed to be a major cause of high blood pressure which can lead to heart disease and strokes. It is estimated that reducing salt intake to no more than 6 g a day for adults and 4 g a day for children could mean that fewer than 20 per cent of people would suffer strokes and there would be 15 per cent fewer heart attacks – saving 40,000 lives each year.

Sugar

Children eat twice as much sugar as they should and sugar can come in many different disguises.

Those ending in 'ose' are sugars, e.g. glucose, fructose, sucrose, maltose, dextrose. Also: honey, maple syrup, fruit syrup, molasses, corn syrup, mannitol and sorbitol.

A high sugar intake can upset the blood sugar balance – the amount of sugar that is in the blood stream. Blood sugar highs and lows can trigger energy and mood swings, hyperactivity and can also affect a child's concentration. If their blood sugar levels are rapidly rising and crashing children can be left feeling irritable and exhausted which can then affect the quality of their sleep.

To reduce the sugar 'hit', choose drinks that are 100 per cent fruit juice and dilute them with still or sparkling water. Avoid anything that is labelled as 'fruit drink' or 'fruit juice drink' as this may contain as little as 10 per cent fruit juice and many can include 5 teaspoons of sugar in a single glass. Not only will there be additives, but this works out to be a very expensive way of drinking fruit juice. Avoid fizzy drinks, too, as these are even worse and can contain 7 to 8 teaspoons of sugar in a single can.

It is important to wean children off sugary products as soon as possible in order to re-educate their tastebuds. Home-made puddings and cookies generally contain much less added sugar than commercially made ones, so it's another reason to make your own whenever possible.

One of the biggest problems caused by too much sugar in children's diets is dental decay. Try to confine sugary foods to mealtimes – not only to reduce the frequency of eating sugary foods but also because eating other foods at the same time dilutes the acid and reduces the harmful effects of the sugar. There is also more saliva present in the mouth to wash the acids away.

Checking the label
As a rule, look for food and drink with less than 2 g of sugar per serving, as these foods are low in sugar. Anything containing more than 10 g of sugar per serving counts as being high in sugar.

Foods for energy

To stay on top both physically and mentally you should eat several servings of carbohydrates a day – preferably unrefined foods like pasta, wholegrain cereals and bread, pulses and baked potatoes. The fibre in these foods slows down the rate at which sugar is released, providing a steady supply of energy.

Oats have an especially slow rate of energy release, so a bowl of porridge makes a good breakfast and oatmeal and raisin cookies are a high-energy snack (see page 168 for my recipe). Bananas are another good energy-boosting snack.

Dehydration is another common cause of lethargy, so watch your fluid intake.

Brain-boosting foods

The right combination of foodstuffs can boost the brain as well as the body. Iron and essential fatty acids are particularly important:

Iron
The highest concentration of iron is found in the brain and therefore an adequate intake is crucial for proper brain development. (See page 8 for information on iron.)

Foods containing iron have been shown to prevent anaemia, a condition that leads to tiredness, decreased mental alertness, lowered IQ and overall apathy. This is because when iron stores are low, less of the oxygen carrying the pigment haemoglobin is made and so less oxygen gets to the brain – resulting in difficulty concentrating and a shortened attention span.

Essential fatty acids
Oil-rich fish such as salmon and sardines are especially good brain boosters, due to their high levels of Omega-3 essential fatty acids. These EFAs are vital for brain function and can be of particular benefit to dyslexic, dyspraxic and hyperactive children. (See page 8 for more information on EFAs.)

Boosting brain power with complex carbohydrates

Carbohydrates provide the body and the brain's main source of energy, so in order to boost brain power it is important for your child to eat a breakfast that includes some complex (unrefined) carbohydrates. If your child has a bowl of sugary cereal or white bread with chocolate spread or jam first thing in the morning, the sugar is digested very rapidly and his blood sugar level will shoot up. But this high rise will, within an hour, be followed by a rapid drop in blood sugar which in turn leads to dips in energy and hunger. This dip can trigger poor concentration, erratic learning, disruptive behaviour and fatigue.

The best way to deliver a steady supply of sugar to the brain is to give your child complex carbohydrates such as wholemeal bread, wholegrain cereals, pasta or fruit. These consist of slowly digested carbohydrates and the fibre contained in these foods helps slow down the rate at which sugar is released, giving longer-lasting concentration and sustained energy.

The right mix of protein foods and slow-releasing carbohydrates will help to ward off the typical afternoon energy slump.

Brain-boosting snacks

These are just a few ideas for food you can give your child to start the day, or to snack on to keep up their concentration.

- Creamy scrambled eggs on wholemeal toast.
- Bowl of blueberries or a banana.
- Iron-enriched breakfast cereal topped with chopped fresh fruit.
- Dried fruit, e.g. raisins or apricots.
- Toasted raisin bread spread with peanut butter.
- Pasta salad with chicken, sweetcorn, cherry tomatoes and spring onion.
- Crudités (think colourful, traffic light colours), with dips such as hummus.
- Wholemeal crackers or oatcakes with peanut butter or dips.
- Fresh fruit with live natural yoghurt and cinnamon to sweeten.
- Pitta bread stuffed with turkey and salad or tuna mayo with sweetcorn and spring onion.

Eggs

Eggs are packed with goodness; after all, they contain all the nutrients to support a new chick. They are also rich in choline – a B vitamin contained in the egg yolk that is a key component in the brain transmitter called 'acetylcholine'. This is crucial for good memory function.

Water

Keep hydrated. Studies show that children who drink lots of water are better at concentrating, taking in information and mental arithmetic.

Fruit juice, milk and tea count towards fluid intake but plain water is best. Get children into the habit of taking a bottle of water to school with them every day.

What to eat for an exam

On exam day it's even more important that children have the best start for the day. Even if nerves are getting the better of them, try to get them to eat something.

• A protein-rich breakfast, e.g. scrambled eggs, beans or cheese on toast, a banana and yoghurt.
• Take a bottle of water into the exam room.
• A banana 15 minutes before the exam will boost staying power.

Avoid sugar, chocolates, sweets, biscuits and other foods that are high in sugar. You might think they will give you an energy boost, but it's short-lived and can leave you feeling more tired than before.

Spring Menu Planner

Monday

AFTER-SCHOOL SNACKS
Prawn and watercress sandwiches (p36)
Power-packed oat bars with cranberries,
  apricots and pumpkin seeds (p178)

SUPPER
Chicken satay with rice (p93)
Fresh fruit ice lollies (pp161–3)

Tuesday

AFTER-SCHOOL SNACKS
Toasted ham and cheese muffin (p25)
Chewy oatmeal raisin cookies (p168)

SUPPER
Annabel's Pad Thai noodles (p62)
Simple berry fruit brulée (p148)

Wednesday

AFTER-SCHOOL SNACKS
Chopped Cobb salad (p34)
Dried fruit, e.g. raisins, apricots

SUPPER
Kid's chicken curry with rice (p101)
Caramel bananas (p158)

Thursday

AFTER-SCHOOL SNACKS
Stuffed pitta pocket with tuna, egg and
  sweetcorn (p24)
Fruit

SUPPER
Evelyn's meatballs with sweet and sour sauce
  (p110)
Raspberry ripple dessert (p150)

Friday

AFTER-SCHOOL SNACKS
Pasta shell salad with chicken and sweetcorn
  (p32)
Annabel's peanut butter balls
  (p180)

SUPPER
Goujons of fish with tartare sauce (p80)
Summer berry yoghurt ice cream or Luscious
  lychee frozen yoghurt (p156)

Summer Menu Planner

Monday

AFTER-SCHOOL SNACKS

Chicken Caesar wrap (p18)

Fruit kebabs (p38)

SUPPER

Spaghetti primavera (p142)

Mango and strawberries with passion fruit
  sauce (p147)

Tuesday

AFTER-SCHOOL SNACKS

Power-packed oat bars with cranberries,
  apricots and pumpkin seeds (p178)

Fruit smoothie (p46)

SUPPER

Finger pickin' chicken balls (p92)

Broccoli and carrots

Fruity cranberry and lemonade jellies (p153)

Wednesday

AFTER-SCHOOL SNACKS

Salad kebabs (p38)

Apricot and white chocolate Rice Krispie
  squares (p175)

SUPPER

Chinese-style fish fillets (p75)

Fresh fruit ice lollies (pp161–3)

Thursday

AFTER-SCHOOL SNACKS

Pasta salad with prawns (p37)

Fruit

SUPPER

Sesame beef stir fry (p116)

Fruit and frozen yoghurt

Friday

AFTER-SCHOOL SNACKS

Little gem cups (p40)

Oat, raisin and sunflower seed cookies (p45)

SUPPER

Chicken on the griddle (p102)

Corn on the cob

Amaretto and summer fruit gratin (p155)

Autumn Menu Planner

Monday

AFTER-SCHOOL SNACKS
Tuna melt (p27)
Fruit

SUPPER
Annabel's Bolognese (p117)
Simple berry fruit brulée (p148)

Tuesday

AFTER-SCHOOL SNACKS
Chinese chicken wrap (p20)
Yogurt

SUPPER
Tasty salmon and spinach pie (p85)
Rhubarb and strawberry crumble (p154)

Wednesday

AFTER-SCHOOL SNACKS
Salad kebabs (p38)
Chewy oatmeal raisin cookies (p168)

SUPPER
Caroline's turkey meatballs with spaghetti and
   tomato sauce (p66)
Eton mess (p159)

Thursday

AFTER-SCHOOL SNACKS
Mini pitta pizzas (p29)
Fruit

SUPPER
Butternut squash, carrot and ginger soup
   (p128)
Annabel's chicken dippers (p94)

Friday

AFTER-SCHOOL SNACKS
Carrot and cucumber sticks with hummus
Apple and carrot muffins (p42)

SUPPER
Baked risotto with tomato, courgette and
   Parmesan (p137)
Summer berry yoghurt ice cream or Luscious
   lychee frozen yoghurt (p156)

Winter Menu Planner

Monday

AFTER-SCHOOL SNACKS
Welsh rarebit (p27)
Fruit

SUPPER
Nicholas's multi-layered cottage pie (p115)
Ruby fruit salad (p155)

Tuesday

AFTER-SCHOOL SNACKS
Apple and raisin bran muffin (p45)
Fruit smoothie (p46)

SUPPER
Honey and soy salmon kebabs (p71)
Cheesy baked potato (p139)
Fruit

Wednesday

AFTER-SCHOOL SNACKS
Golden lentil and vegetable soup (p129)
Tomato and mozzarella salad (p31)

SUPPER
Jacques' sesame chicken fingers with chips
   (p90)
Lara's favourite brownies (p173)

Thursday

AFTER-SCHOOL SNACKS
Crumpet pizzas (p28)
Fromage frais and fruit

SUPPER
Annabel's paella (p77)
Apple, blackberry and pear crumble (p151)

Friday

AFTER-SCHOOL SNACKS
Mexican egg wrap (p19)
Fruit kebabs (p38)

SUPPER
Scarlett's spaghettini with chicken, tomatoes
   and basil (p50)
Honey-layered yoghurt with blueberries and
   raspberries (p147)

1 Savoury snacks, sweet treats

Chicken Caesar wrap

Wraps make a nice change from ordinary sandwiches and if you put the fillings into several bowls children will have fun making them up themselves. This version uses the classic Caesar dressing with chicken. As a shortcut you could use a bought Caesar salad dressing to mix with the chicken.

DRESSING

1¹/₂ tbsp mayonnaise

1 tsp water

small squeeze of lemon juice

a few drops Worcestershire sauce

1¹/₂ tsp freshly grated Parmesan cheese

1 tortilla

40 g (1¹/₂ oz) cooked chicken, shredded

2 tbsp grated carrot

15 g (¹/₂ oz) shredded lettuce

Mix together the mayonnaise, water, squeeze of lemon, Worcestershire sauce and Parmesan to make the dressing. Heat the tortilla for 20 seconds in a microwave or heat for about 15 seconds each side in a dry frying pan.

Mix together the cooked chicken and grated carrot and toss with the dressing. Arrange the chicken in a line near one end of the tortilla. Top with the shredded lettuce and roll up.

Makes 1 portion

Prawn and lettuce wrap

If you don't have sweet chilli sauce, you can mix the mayonnaise together with a little ketchup and Worcestershire sauce instead.

1¹/₂ tbsp mayonnaise

³/₄ tsp sweet chilli sauce

small squeeze lemon juice

50 g (2 oz) small cooked prawns

1 tortilla

**a little shredded iceberg lettuce
(about 10 g/¹/₂ oz)**

Mix together the mayonnaise, sweet chilli sauce and squeeze of lemon. Stir in the prawns. Heat the tortilla for 20 seconds in a microwave or heat for about 15 seconds each side in a dry frying pan.

Arrange the prawns near one end of the tortilla, cover with the shredded lettuce and roll up. Cut the tortilla in half diagonally.

Makes 1 portion

Chicken wrap with tomato pesto

You can use red pesto or sun-dried tomato paste in this, and instead of chopped fresh tomato you could add 2 chopped sunblush tomatoes.

1–1¹/₂ tbsp mayonnaise

¹/₂ tsp red pesto or sun-dried tomato paste

small squeeze of lemon juice

40 g (1¹/₂ oz) cooked chicken, shredded

¹/₂ tomato, diced

1 tortilla

15 g (¹/₂ oz) shredded iceberg lettuce

Mix together the mayonnaise, pesto and lemon juice. Stir in the cooked chicken and diced tomato. Heat the tortilla.

Arrange the chicken near one end of the tortilla, cover with shredded lettuce and roll up. Cut the tortilla in half diagonally.

Makes 1 portion

Mexican egg wrap

Scrambled eggs with a little kick are great served inside a warm tortilla. A fun way to find out whether eggs are fresh is to place the egg in a glass of water; if it stays at the bottom it is very fresh, but if tilts up slightly it is up to a week old. If it floats – throw it away.

15 g (¹/₂ oz) butter

2 level tsp chopped onion

2 level tsp chopped red pepper

1 large egg

1 tbsp milk

a few drops Tabasco, to taste

a little salt and white pepper

1 tortilla

Melt the butter until foaming. Fry the onion and pepper for about 5 minutes or until soft. Beat the egg with the milk, Tabasco and seasoning and cook over a low heat, stirring gently until scrambled. Heat the tortilla for 20 seconds in a microwave or heat for about 15 seconds each side in a dry frying pan.

Spoon the scrambled egg near one end of the tortilla and roll up. Cut in half diagonally.

Makes 1 portion

Savoury snacks, sweet treats

Chinese chicken wrap

This is one of my favourite fillings for a wrap – it's a sort of cheat's version
of Chinese duck in pancakes. It provides a good mix of low fat protein and
complex carbs and also useful amounts of B vitamins and iron.

$1^1/_2$ **tbsp mayonnaise**

$^1/_2$ **tsp soy sauce**

1 tsp plum sauce

40 g ($1^1/_2$ oz) cooked chicken, shredded

25 g (1 oz) peeled cucumber, cut into
  matchsticks

$^1/_2$ **tsp toasted sesame seeds (optional)**

1 tortilla

Mix together the mayonnaise, soy sauce and plum
sauce. Stir in the shredded chicken and cucumber.
Sprinkle over the toasted sesame seeds (if using).

Heat the tortilla (as in previous recipe). Arrange
the filling near one end of the tortilla and roll up.

Makes 1 portion

*Opposite: Chinese chicken wrap, Prawn
and lettuce wrap, Mexican egg wrap*

Cream cheese, banana and honey wrap

This is also delicious if you mix the cream cheese together with Dulce de Leche – a delicious caramel spread that you can buy in jars in most supermarkets.

1 tortilla

25 g (1 oz) cream cheese (e.g. Philadelphia cheese)

¹/₂ tsp runny honey or 1 tsp Dulce de Leche

1 small banana, peeled and sliced

Warm the tortilla for 20 seconds in a microwave. Mix together the cream cheese and honey and spread over half the tortilla, it will melt slightly as the tortilla is warm. Arrange the sliced banana on top and roll up.

Makes 1 portion

Dominic's hummus and ham pitta pockets

Dominic is the lucky guy who is married to the *Masterchef 2005* runner-up, Caroline Brewester. This is what he likes to eat for lunch on Saturday; I don't think Caroline has much trouble in whipping this up for him, she's a very talented chef.

1 pitta bread

2 tbsp hummus

25 g (1 oz) wafer thin ham

15 g (¹/₂ oz) iceberg lettuce, shredded

a little black pepper

Toast the pitta bread, cut in half and split open. Spread a tablespoon of hummus on either side. Fold up the ham and stuff into the pitta. Fill the top with the shredded lettuce and season with a little black pepper.

Makes 1 portion

Carrots are a powerhouse of plant pigments, one of which is betacarotene; it is this pigment that the body converts to vitamin A when it is needed. The body uses vitamin A to grow and repair cells and tissue, including those found in the skin, so it can help keep skin soft and smooth and aid in healing. It also works to protect the lining of the stomach, lungs, nose and eyelids, helping to keep out any nasty invading bacteria. Carrots contain more sugar than most other vegetables and they become sweeter when cooked.

Pitta pocket with hummus and carrot

Hummus and carrot is another good combination in pitta bread, and makes a particularly good vegetarian option. Hummus is a good source of low GI carbs, which means that it helps to balance blood sugars. It also provides good amounts of protein and fibre, particularly the soluble variety that helps lower blood cholesterol. Choosing wholegrain pitta instead of white will boost the content of insoluble fibre.

1 pitta bread

3 tbsp hummus

1 large carrot, peeled and grated

Toast the pitta bread, cut in half and split open. Spread one and a half tablespoons of hummus on either side and fill with the grated carrot.

Makes 1 portion

Stuffed pitta pocket with tuna, egg and sweetcorn

Pitta pockets stuffed with a nutritious filling make a good snack or light lunch. This tuna mix is very tasty. Tuna and sweetcorn is a classic combination but it's also a very nutritious one because the egg and tuna provide protein, B vitamins and some iron while the sweetcorn provides fibre, vitamin C and betacarotene.

2 eggs
1 x 200 g (7 oz) can tuna in oil
100 g (4 oz) sweetcorn
2 tbsp mayonnaise
1 tsp white wine vinegar
4 spring onions, chopped
salt and freshly ground black pepper
a few drops Tabasco sauce
salad cress (optional)
2 pitta breads

Put the eggs in a saucepan of cold water and bring to the boil. Reduce the heat and simmer for 7 to 8 minutes (the yolk should be solid). Drain and cool under cold water. Peel the eggs when cold.

Meanwhile, strain the oil from the can of tuna and mix the flaked tuna together with the sweetcorn, mayonnaise, white wine vinegar, spring onions, salt and pepper and the Tabasco sauce. Roughly chop the hard-boiled eggs and add to the tuna mix with the salad cress (if using), stirring well.

Toast the pitta bread, cut in half to give 4 pitta pockets and divide the mixture between them.

Makes 2 portions

Toasted ham and cheese muffin

Instead of sprinkling the ham with Worcestershire sauce, you can spread the muffins thinly with mustard, then top with ham and cheese and grill until golden.

1 English muffin

a little margarine or butter

25 g (1 oz) wafer thin ham

a few drops Worcestershire sauce

25 g (1 oz) Cheddar cheese, grated

Preheat the grill to medium. Split the muffin and arrange the two halves upside down on a grill pan and grill for one minute.

Remove, turn over and spread with a little margarine or butter. Divide the ham between the two slices and add a few drops of Worcestershire sauce. Top with the grated cheese and grill for 3 to 4 minutes until golden.

Makes 1 portion

Muffins with creamy scrambled eggs

2 English muffins

4 eggs

3 tbsp single cream

a little salt and freshly ground black pepper

15 g (^{1}/$_2$ oz) butter

OPTIONAL EXTRAS

snipped chives

thin strips smoked salmon

chopped tomato

strips of ham

Split the muffins and toast them. Meanwhile, break the eggs into a small bowl, add the cream and season with salt and pepper. Whisk lightly. Melt the butter in a heavy-bottomed, non-stick saucepan over a medium heat. Pour in the egg mixture, leave for a few seconds and then stir briskly with a wooden spoon until softly set. At this stage you can stir in one of the optional extras.

Spread the split muffins with a little butter and pile the scrambled eggs on top.

Makes 2 portions

Cheesy muffins

Delicious savoury muffins. As a variation you could make cheese and sweet-corn muffins by adding 2 tbsp maple syrup to the milk mixture, increasing the cheese quantity to 100 g (4 oz), using 5 spring onions and then stirring in 75 g (3 oz) tinned sweetcorn.

50 ml (2 fl oz) milk

50 ml (2 fl oz) vegetable oil

125 ml (4 fl oz) natural yoghurt

2 eggs

185 g (6^1/$_2$ oz) plain flour

1^1/$_2$ tsp baking powder

^{1}/$_2$ tsp bicarbonate of soda

^{1}/$_4$ tsp paprika

^{1}/$_2$ tsp salt and freshly ground black pepper

85 g (3^1/$_2$ oz) Cheddar cheese, grated

4 spring onions, sliced

75 g (3 oz) sunblush tomatoes, chopped

40 g (1^1/$_2$ oz) freshly grated Parmesan
  cheese, for the topping

Pre-heat the oven to 180°C/350°F/Gas Mark 4. Combine the milk, oil, yoghurt and eggs in a jug. In a separate bowl, sift together the plain flour, baking powder, bicarbonate of soda, paprika, salt and pepper. Stir in the Cheddar cheese, spring onions and sunblush tomatoes.

Add the liquid ingredients and mix quickly before spooning into a muffin tray lined with paper cases. Sprinkle the Parmesan on top and bake in the oven for 20 minutes.

Makes 10 muffins

SUPERFOOD TIP
Cheese

Cheese is a great source of vegetarian protein that also provides calcium for the growth of healthy bones and teeth. Calcium in dairy products is more easily absorbed by the body than from other foods. Growing children are recommended to have 3-4 servings from the dairy group each day. Cheese also contains moderate levels of zinc, which is needed for strong immune systems and our senses of smell and taste. Cheese is a source of tryptophan, too, which the body converts to serotonin to make us feel happy and in a good mood.

Savoury snacks, sweet treats

Tuna melt

This is quick, easy and nutritious and my children love it. If you don't have
crème fraîche you could use Greek yoghurt instead.

200 g (7 oz) can tuna in water
2 tbsp tomato ketchup
2 tbsp crème fraîche
1 or 2 finely sliced spring onions
2 English muffins
40 g (1¹/₂ oz) Cheddar cheese, grated

Drain the water from the tuna and flake into
small pieces. Mix together with the tomato
ketchup, crème fraîche and spring onions.

Split the muffins and toast them. Spread with the
tuna mixture and sprinkle with the grated Cheddar.
Place the muffins under a pre-heated grill and
grill until the cheese is golden and bubbling.

Makes 2 portions

Welsh rarebit

This is the perfect mixture for a really tasty Welsh rarebit. Traditionally Welsh
rarebit is flavoured with beer, but you can use milk instead. To make fresh
breadcrumbs, simply tear a slice of white bread into pieces and whizz in a
food processor. You could also spread this mixture onto toast.

150 g (5 oz) grated mature Cheddar cheese
2 tbsp milk (or beer)
a few drops Worcestershire sauce
a generous pinch dried mustard powder
3 tbsp fresh white breadcrumbs
1 small egg yolk, lightly beaten
2 English muffins
paprika

Pre-heat the grill to hot. Place the cheese and
milk in a saucepan over a low heat, stirring until
melted. Add the Worcestershire sauce and
mustard powder. Remove from the heat, stir in the
breadcrumbs and beaten egg yolk. Split and toast
the muffins and spread with the rarebit topping.
Sprinkle with paprika. Cook under the grill until
golden and bubbling (1 to 2 minutes).

Makes 4 muffins

Toasted crumpets with banana and peanut butter

Peanut butter is rich in unsaturated fats that help to keep the heart healthy.
Combined with honey and banana it makes a tasty, nutritious and filling snack.

2 crumpets
2 tbsp peanut butter
a little honey
1 small banana, sliced

Toast the crumpets under a preheated grill. Remove and spread with peanut butter. Drizzle over a little honey and arrange the sliced banana on top. Place on a tray under a preheated grill again for a couple of minutes.

Makes 1 portion

Crumpet pizzas

Crumpets make a yummy pizza base. You can make up the tomato sauce and it will keep in the fridge for several days. You can also add toppings, like ham.

2 tbsp olive oil
1 small onion, chopped
large pinch of sugar
1 tsp tomato purée
200 g (7 oz) tinned chopped tomatoes
pinch of dried oregano
1/2 tsp balsamic vinegar
salt and freshly ground black pepper
4 crumpets
50 g (2 oz) Cheddar cheese, grated

Heat the oil in a frying pan, add the chopped onion and sugar and sauté for 2 to 3 minutes. Stir in the tomato purée. Add the chopped tomatoes, oregano, balsamic vinegar and seasoning. Simmer for 5 to 6 minutes until thickened and season again to taste.

Preheat the grill and toast the crumpets on each side, or you can put them in the toaster. Divide the tomato sauce between the crumpets, top with the grated cheese and cook under the grill for 2 to 3 minutes until golden.

Makes 4 portions

Ham and pineapple pizzas

Ready-rolled puff pastry from the supermarket makes a good base for these delicious pizzas.

250 g (9 oz) ready-rolled puff pastry

4 tsp tomato purée

4 tsp red pesto

25 g (1 oz) honey roast, wafer thin ham

60 g (2¹/₂ oz) tinned pineapple chunks

85 g (3¹/₂ oz) mozzarella, torn into pieces

salt and freshly ground black pepper

Unroll the puff pastry and cut out 4 x 12cm (5in) diameter circles, or cut around a saucer using a sharp knife. Place the puff pastry pizza bases on a baking sheet. Using the knife, score a circle 5mm (¹/₄ in) from the edge of the pastry to form a rim.

Mix together the tomato purée and pesto and spread over the base of the pizzas, inside the rim. Divide the ham and the pineapple between the pizza bases and scatter over the mozzarella. Season to taste. Bake in a pre-heated oven at 200°C/400°F/Gas Mark 6 for 10 to 15 minutes.

Makes 4 small pizzas

Mini pitta pizzas

Mini round pitta breads or split and toasted English muffins make a good base for these individual pizzas. You can vary the toppings, maybe adding extras such as sliced mushrooms, strips of ham or pepperoni.

4 mini, round pitta breads

4 tbsp pizza sauce

2 spring onions, finely sliced

4 tbsp tinned sweetcorn

8 cherry tomatoes, sliced

salt and freshly ground black pepper

75 g (3 oz) mixed, ready-grated Cheddar and mozzarella, or just grated Cheddar

a little olive oil

4 sprigs of basil (optional)

Arrange the pitta breads on a baking sheet and spread with the pizza sauce. Sprinkle over the spring onions, sweetcorn and sliced cherry tomatoes, season with a little salt and pepper and top with the grated cheeses. Drizzle over a little olive oil.

Bake in an oven pre-heated to 180°C/350°F/Gas Mark 4, for about 10 minutes. Decorate with some sprigs of fresh basil.

Makes 4 pizzas

Tomato and mozzarella salad

Mozzarella and tomato salad is always popular. Mozzarella has a delicious creamy taste that most children love and it also provides useful amounts of calcium, protein and several of the B vitamins. I have added some roasted pine nuts to this dish, but you could leave these out if your child prefers.

2 tbsp pine nuts

75 g (3 oz) fusilli pasta

100 g (4 oz) baby plum tomatoes

2 tbsp basil leaves, torn into pieces

60 g (2^1/$_2$ oz) mozzarella (half of a 125 g/4^1/$_2$ oz ball), cubed or use mini mozzarella balls

DRESSING

3 tbsp olive oil

2 tsp balsamic vinegar

salt and freshly ground black pepper

Toast the pine nuts in an oven preheated to 180°C/350°F/Gas Mark 4 for 15 minutes. Alternatively, sauté them for a couple of minutes, stirring until golden in a dry frying pan.

Cook the fusilli in a pan of lightly salted boiling water for 12 minutes, or according to the packet instructions. Drain and run under cold running water. Mix together the pasta, pine nuts, tomatoes, basil and mozzarella. Make the dressing by whisking together the oil and vinegar and adding salt and pepper. Toss the salad in the dressing.

Makes 2 portions

Pasta shell salad with chicken and sweetcorn

Sweetcorn is a useful source of several of the B vitamins, especially folate. It also provides good amounts of fibre, vitamin C and potassium. It's handy to have a bowl of this salad in the fridge for your children to help themselves to when they feel hungry. If you want to save time use ready-cooked chicken or turkey in this dish instead.

1 large chicken breast (approx. 125 g/4$^{1}/_{2}$ oz)

300 ml ($^{1}/_{2}$ pint) chicken stock

150 g (5 oz) tiny shell pasta

100 g (4 oz) fine green beans

100 g (4 oz) tinned sweetcorn

3 spring onions, finely chopped (optional)

DRESSING

4 tbsp light olive oil

1 tbsp balsamic vinegar

1 tbsp soy sauce

$^{1}/_{2}$ tsp caster sugar

a little freshly ground black pepper and salt

Poach the chicken in the chicken stock for 7 to 8 minutes, or until cooked through. Remove with a slotted spoon and allow to cool a little. When cool, shred the chicken into pieces.

Cook the pasta according to the instructions on the packet and steam the green beans for about 5 minutes, or until tender but still crunchy. Drain the cooked pasta and mix together with the shredded chicken, green beans, sweetcorn and spring onions (if using).

Whisk together all the ingredients for the dressing and toss with the pasta salad.

Makes 4 portions

S U P E R F O O D   T I P
Sweetcorn

Sweetcorn is an excellent source of B vitamins, which are needed for energy production. It also contains plenty of fibre to keep the digestive system in good working order. It contains the antioxidant zeaxanthin (in greater amounts when cooked) which helps protect the retinas of the eyes.

Pasta and chicken salad with honey and soy vinaigrette

The honey soy dressing gives this simple salad a flavour children will love. The cherry tomatoes and sweetcorn provide vitamin C, fibre and phytochemicals that help to keep the heart healthy.

100 g (4 oz) pasta

1 tbsp vegetable oil

1 shallot

1 chicken breast, cut into bite-sized pieces

198 g (7 oz) can sweetcorn

6 cherry tomatoes (approx. 75 g/3 oz), halved

1 spring onion, finely sliced

VINAIGRETTE

3 tbsp light olive oil

1 tbsp runny honey

1 tbsp soy sauce

1 tbsp lemon juice

Cook the pasta in lightly salted boiling water, according to the instructions on the packet. Heat the vegetable oil in a pan and sauté the shallot for 2 minutes. Add the chicken and sauté until cooked. Combine the drained pasta, chicken, sweetcorn, cherry tomatoes and spring onion in a bowl.

Whisk together the ingredients for the dressing and toss with the salad.

Makes 3 portions

Chopped Cobb salad

This is good served in a glass bowl so that the colourful layers show up well. You could also make individual portions in glasses. You can use other ingredients depending on what your child likes. I like to include avocado if I am making this for myself. In the USA this is usually made with Roquefort cheese and crumbled crispy bacon, but I think that's a little strong for children.

3 hard-boiled eggs

50 g (2 oz) lettuce, shredded

50 g (2 oz) carrot, grated

1 cooked chicken breast, diced (or use chopped turkey breast)

85 g (3¹/₂ oz) tinned sweetcorn

2 small spring onions, sliced

60 g (2¹/₂ oz) Red Leicester cheese, grated

3 tomatoes, skinned and chopped

DRESSING

1 tbsp white wine vinegar

4 tbsp olive oil

¹/₄ tsp Dijon mustard

¹/₂ tsp caster sugar

1 tbsp double cream

salt and freshly ground black pepper

Remove the shells from the boiled eggs. Chop the egg whites and sieve the egg yolks. Layer up the salad in a flat-bottomed glass bowl in the order given, with the shredded lettuce first, then the grated carrot and so on. Add the remaining layers and then cover with the chopped egg white and top with the sieved egg yolk.

To make the dressing, whisk together the vinegar, oil, mustard and sugar. Finally, whisk in the double cream and season to taste. Pour over the assembled salad.

Makes 3 portions

1

Granary Bread

Providing energy-giving complex carbohydrates and B vitamins needed to release the energy from foods, granary bread is fibre-rich and filling, with a delicious nutty flavour. Wholegrains contain a range of vitamins and minerals to keep us fit and healthy, and wheat is rich in the mineral magnesium which helps to build strong bones and teeth.

Prawn and watercress sandwiches

These are delicious, quick and easy to prepare, and the sandwiches look good cut into triangles and standing up in a row. Gram for gram, watercress contains 12 times more vitamin C than lettuce, and more iron than spinach. It contains good amounts of the vitamins C, B6 and folate and useful amounts of the minerals magnesium, iron and potassium.

4 slices granary bread

soft margarine or softened butter

a handful of watercress, trimmed, tough stalks removed

125 g (4¹/₂ oz) cooked prawns

2 tbsp mayonnaise

1 tbsp tomato ketchup

paprika

Spread two slices of bread with margarine or softened butter. Arrange the watercress on the bread. Mix the prawns together with the mayonnaise and ketchup and spoon onto the watercress. Sprinkle with paprika and sandwich together with the remaining bread. Trim the crusts and cut into quarters.

Makes 2 portions

Pasta salad with prawns

125 g (4½ oz) pasta shapes
125 g (4½ oz) cooked prawns
½ avocado, peeled and chopped
6 cherry tomatoes, cut in half
½ little gem lettuce, shredded

DRESSING
3 tbsp mayonnaise
1 tbsp tomato ketchup
dash of Worcestershire sauce
squeeze of lemon juice

a little paprika

Cook the pasta in boiling, lightly salted water, according to the instructions on the packet. Put the prawns, avocado, cherry tomatoes and shredded lettuce into a bowl together with the drained, cooked pasta.

Mix together the mayonnaise, tomato ketchup, Worcestershire sauce and lemon juice and toss the salad with the dressing. Sprinkle over a little paprika.

Makes 2 portions

Chef's salad

1 little gem lettuce, finely sliced
8 cherry tomatoes, cut in half
100 g (4 oz) cooked turkey breast,
 cut into cubes
100 g (4 oz) tinned or cooked,
 frozen sweetcorn
50 g (2 oz) Swiss cheese, cut into
 small cubes

HONEY AND SOY DRESSING
3 tbsp light olive oil
1 tbsp runny honey
1 tbsp soy sauce
1 tbsp fresh lemon juice

or

THOUSAND ISLAND DRESSING
1 tbsp tomato ketchup
½ tsp soy sauce
a few drops Worcestershire sauce
2 tbsp double cream
2 tbsp mayonnaise
squeeze of lemon juice

Whisk together the ingredients for the dressing of your choice. Put the salad ingredients into a bowl and toss with the dressing.

Makes 4 portions

1

Salad kebabs

These can be savoury or sweet. For the sticks you can use bamboo skewers or thin plastic straws. Here are some suggestions for food combinations to thread onto the skewers.

- **Slices of ham or turkey rolled up and interspersed with cubes of cheese and wedges of pineapple.**

- **Cherry tomatoes and mozzarella cheese.**

- **Cucumber, carrot, red pepper and cubes of Gruyère or Emmenthal cheese.**

- **Chicken tikka pieces with cucumber.**

Fruit kebabs

You can also make fruit kebabs by threading bite-sized pieces of fruit onto a skewer. As a treat you could include chocolate-dipped fruit. Choose from:

- **Chunks of pineapple.**

- **Dried apricots.**

- **Strawberries.**

- **Melon balls.**

- **Kiwi.**

- **Grapes.**

- **Mango chunks.**

Little gem cups

Instead of sandwiches you can use the boat-shaped leaves of little gem lettuce to hold delicious fillings. This version uses ham and pineapple.

¹/₂ tsp pineapple juice, from the tin
1 tbsp mayonnaise
25 g (1 oz) shredded ham or chicken
1 pineapple ring, cut into small pieces
2 outer gem lettuce leaves

Mix together the half teaspoon of pineapple juice and the mayonnaise. Combine the shredded ham and diced pineapple and mix with the mayonnaise. Spoon into the lettuce leaves.

Makes 2 portions

Saucy chicken gems

1 cooked chicken breast, without skin
1 little gem lettuce
8 tsp tomato salsa
4 tsp sour cream or low-fat yogurt

Cut the chicken into small bite-sized pieces. Separate the lettuce leaves and choose 8 that are a good size. Wash and shake dry, then fill with chicken and top with salsa and sour cream or yogurt.

Makes 8 portions

Other filling ideas:

- Diced chicken and canned apricot mixed with yoghurt, a little mild curry paste and honey.
- 1 rasher streaky bacon, grilled and drained on kitchen paper. Mix with 4 diced cherry tomatoes and a little mayonnaise.
- Diced Edam cheese and red apple, mixed with an equal amount of mayonnaise and yoghurt.
- Small cooked prawns mixed with mayonnaise and a little fresh lemon juice.

- Grated carrots, raisins and mayonnaise.
- Small cooked prawns mixed with mayonnaise, tomato ketchup and chopped watercress.
- Flaked, tinned tuna mixed with low fat crème fraîche, a little tomato ketchup and sliced spring onion.
- Diced chicken, sweetcorn, mayonnaise and spring onions.

Savoury snacks, sweet treats

Courgette raisin muffins

This is a delicious way to get your child to eat more vegetables! The grated courgette makes these muffins lovely and moist.

100 g (4 oz) white self-raising flour

100 g (4 oz) soft brown sugar

$^1/_2$ tsp mixed spice

$^1/_2$ tsp baking powder

pinch of salt

100 g (4 oz) wholemeal self-raising flour

180 ml (6 fl oz) milk

85 g ($3^1/_2$ oz) melted butter

1 egg, lightly beaten

100 g (4 oz) raisins

1 tsp soft brown sugar

Sieve together the white flour, sugar, mixed spice, baking powder and salt. Then sift in the whole-meal flour, saving the bran bits in the sieve. Mix together the milk, melted butter and egg. Add the liquid to the flour mixture and stir in the raisins.

Line a muffin tray with 12 paper cases. Fill each one with the muffin mix until about two-thirds full. Mix together the reserved bran and the soft brown sugar and sprinkle on top of each muffin. Place in an oven pre-heated to 170°C/325°F/Gas Mark 3, and bake for 25 minutes.

Makes 12 muffins

SUPERFOOD TIP
Courgette

Courgette comes from the French word for marrow: *courge*. In the USA they are called zucchini; *zucca* is the Italian word for marrow and *zucchini* means little marrow. Courgettes have tender edible skins and this is where most of the nutrients lie. They are low in calories and a good source of betacarotene.

Apple and carrot muffins with maple syrup

This is one of my favourite muffin recipes, and they are so easy to make. They are great for breakfast, lunchboxes or just a snack. Using wholemeal flour helps to boost the fibre content and adding grated carrot and apple keeps the muffins moist and gives them a delicious fruit flavour.
Suitable for freezing

150 g (5 oz) plain wholemeal flour

50 g (2 oz) granulated sugar

25 g (1 oz) dried skimmed milk powder

1¹/₂ tsp baking powder

¹/₂ tsp cinnamon

¹/₂ tsp ground ginger

¹/₄ tsp salt

125 ml (4¹/₂ fl oz) vegetable oil

50 ml (2 fl oz) honey

50 ml (2 fl oz) maple syrup

2 eggs, lightly beaten

¹/₂ tsp vanilla essence

1 large apple, peeled and grated

75g (3 oz) carrots, peeled and grated

75g (3 oz) raisins

Pre-heat the oven to 180°C/350°F/Gas Mark 4. Combine the flour, sugar, skimmed milk powder, baking powder, cinnamon, ginger and salt in a mixing bowl. In a separate bowl, combine the oil, honey, maple syrup, eggs and vanilla essence. Beat lightly with a balloon whisk until blended. Add the grated apple, carrots and raisins to the liquid mixture and stir until just combined.

Line a muffin tray with paper cups and fill until two-thirds full. Bake for 20 to 25 minutes. You can also make mini muffins – which are ideal for children – and they take about 15 minutes to bake.

Makes 12 large muffins

Apple and raisin bran muffins

Complex carbohydrates satisfy the appetite for longer and provide sustained energy, and these delicious muffins give you a good energy boost any time.

50 g (2 oz) plain wholemeal flour

1¹/₂ tsp baking powder

1 tsp ground ginger

1 tsp mixed spice

40 g (1¹/₂ oz) natural wheat bran

100 g (4 oz) soft brown sugar

1 large apple, peeled and grated

100 g (4 oz) raisins

125 ml (4 fl oz) vegetable oil

2 eggs beaten

2 tbsp honey

1 tbsp maple syrup

2 tbsp milk

Mix together the flour, baking powder, ground ginger, mixed spice, wheat bran and sugar. Add the grated apple and raisins. In a jug, mix together the vegetable oil, beaten egg, honey, maple syrup and milk. Pour into the flour mixture and stir until combined. Spoon into paper-lined muffin cases. Bake in an oven pre-heated to 180°C/350°F/Gas Mark 4 for about 25 minutes until golden.

Makes 10 muffins

Oat, raisin and sunflower seed cookies

This is one of my favourite cookie recipes, and they make a tasty and nutritious snack any time of the day. *Suitable for freezing*

85 g (3¹/₂ oz) butter

75 g (3 oz) soft brown sugar

1 tsp vanilla essence

75 g (3 oz) raisins

40 g (1¹/₂ oz) sunflower seeds

50 g (2 oz) plain flour

75 g (3 oz) porridge oats

¹/₄ tsp bicarbonate of soda

¹/₂ tsp salt

Cream together the butter and sugar until light and fluffy. Stir in all of the remaining ingredients until completely combined. Shape into walnut-sized balls and flatten them onto a non-stick baking tray with your hand. Bake in an oven pre-heated to 180°C/350°F/Gas Mark 4 for about 15 minutes, until they are golden. They will be soft but will harden a little when they are cool.

Makes approx. 14 cookies

Pictured opposite

Smoothies

Peach and banana smoothie

2 ripe juicy peaches
1 small banana
2 tbsp vanilla yoghurt
2 tsp honey
2 tbsp milk

Put the peaches in a small bowl, pour over boiling water and leave for about 30 seconds. Remove and run the peaches under the cold tap. The skins should then peel off easily. Cut the flesh into chunks and blend together with the banana, yoghurt, honey and milk. (*Pictured opposite, left.*)

Makes 2 glasses

Cherry and berry crush

125 g (4¹/₂ oz) cherries
60 g (2¹/₂ oz) each strawberries and raspberries
50 ml (2 fl oz) raspberry drinking yoghurt
4 tsp icing sugar (to taste)

Stone the cherries and blend all the ingredients together. (*Pictured opposite, right.*)

Makes 2 glasses

SUPERFOOD TIP
Cherries

A rich source of the immune-boosting vitamin C and iron that builds healthy red blood cells necessary for energy production, cherries are also packed with antioxidants that can help limit the damage from disease-causing free radicals. Cherries contain powerful anti-cancer properties – ellagic acid, perillyl alcohol and queritrin have been found to inhibit the growth of cancer cells.

Watermelon cocktail

300 g (10 oz) watermelon flesh, cut into chunks
100 ml (3 fl oz) freshly squeezed orange juice
2 tbsp icing sugar

Simply blend together the melon, orange juice and icing sugar. (*Pictured opposite, centre.*)

Makes 2 glasses

Cranberry crush

75 g (3 oz) blueberries
75 g (3 oz) raspberries
100 ml (3 fl oz) cranberry juice
150 ml (¹/₄ pint) strawberry drinking yoghurt

Blitz the blueberries and raspberries in a blender and press through a sieve. Mix together with the cranberry juice and strawberry drinking yoghurt.

Makes 2 glasses

Passion reviver

¹/₂ small mango (75 g/3 oz peeled weight)
300 ml (¹/₂ pint) freshly squeezed orange juice
2 passion fruit
2 tsp honey

Cut the mango into chunks and mix with the orange juice. Sieve the passion fruit and stir in the juice. Add 2 teaspoons of honey and blend with an electric hand blender.

Makes 2 glasses

2 Pasta pronto

Scarlett's spaghettini with chicken, tomatoes and basil

This is really delicious and simple to prepare and it's a particular favourite with my daughter Scarlett, who is addicted to pasta. I like using the semi-dried sunblush tomatoes because they have a rich tomato flavour, whereas fresh tomatoes often lack flavour.

1½ tbsp olive oil

1 onion, finely chopped

1 large clove garlic, crushed

good pinch of chilli flakes

250 g (9 oz) spaghettini

2 chicken breasts (approx. 250 g/9 oz),
  cut into strips

1 tsp fresh thyme leaves

1 tbsp flat leaf parsley, chopped

4 medium tomatoes (295 g/10 oz) skinned,
  de-seeded and roughly chopped

50 g (2 oz) sunblush tomatoes, chopped

350 ml (12 fl oz) chicken stock (use one
  stock cube)

75 g (3 oz) frozen peas

1 tbsp fresh basil leaves, torn

salt and freshly ground black pepper

Heat the oil in a fairly large saucepan and sauté the onion for 3 minutes. Add the garlic and chilli flakes and cook for 2 minutes. Meanwhile, cook the spaghettini according to the instructions on the packet.

Add the chicken to the onion mixture and cook, stirring, for about 4 minutes. Add the thyme and parsley and cook for 1 minute. Add the fresh tomatoes and sunblush tomatoes and cook for 2 minutes. Add the chicken stock, frozen peas and basil and cook for 2 minutes. Add the drained spaghettini and cook, stirring, for 1 minute. Season to taste.

Makes 4–5 portions

SUPERFOOD TIP
Peas

Peas are bursting with nutrients: vegetable protein, fibre for a healthy digestive system and vitamins B and C, along with iron, magnesium and zinc. The mineral magnesium is needed for a healthy heart and works with calcium to build strong bones. The B vitamins are needed to release the energy from food and, with iron, are needed for the formation of red blood cells to carry oxygen. Peas are a great all-round energy-providing food. Frozen peas can be just as nutritious as fresh, because they are frozen within hours of being picked – thus locking in vital nutrients.

Spaghetti with plum and sunblush tomatoes

This is very quick and easy to prepare and tastes delicious. For a good flavour you need to use ripe tomatoes; if the tomatoes are not ripe or lack flavour, add a little tomato purée. *Sauce suitable for freezing*

200 g (7 oz) spaghetti

2 tbsp olive oil

1 onion, chopped

1 clove garlic, crushed

8 ripe plum tomatoes, skinned, de-seeded and chopped (approx. 750 g/24 oz)

100 g (4 oz) sunblush tomatoes

1 tsp balsamic vinegar

handful of basil leaves, torn into pieces

pinch of sugar

salt and freshly ground black pepper

Cook the spaghetti in a large pan of lightly salted water according to the packet instructions. Heat the olive oil in a saucepan and sauté the onion and garlic for 5 to 6 minutes. Add all of the remaining ingredients (except the spaghetti), cover with a lid and cook over a low heat for 10 minutes. Then stir in the cooked spaghetti.

Makes 4 portions

Turkey pasta salad with honey and soy sauce dressing

This salad has a delicious dressing and if you make it for supper it's also good the next day in your child's lunchbox. You can buy moist slices of cooked turkey at the delicatessen counter of the supermarket.

225 g (8 oz) fusilli pasta

125 g (4¹/₂ oz) broccoli, cut into small florets

175 g (6 oz) cherry tomatoes, cut in half

198 g (7 oz) can sweetcorn

150 g (5 oz) cooked turkey, cut into small pieces

4 spring onions, finely sliced

HONEY AND SOY DRESSING

5 tbsp light olive oil

2 tbsp soy sauce

1¹/₂ tbsp honey

1¹/₂ tbsp lemon juice

a little freshly ground black pepper

Cook the pasta according to the packet instructions and steam the broccoli for about 6 minutes or blanch in lightly salted water for a couple of minutes. Meanwhile, whisk together all the ingredients for the dressing. Drain the pasta and combine with the broccoli, cherry tomatoes, sweetcorn, chopped turkey and spring onions in a large bowl. Toss with the dressing and serve.

Makes 4 portions

Pasta twirls with cheese sauce and broccoli

Broccoli is king of the healthy vegetable superstars and to get the best from it
it should be steamed, as boiling almost halves its vitamin content.

40 g (1¹/₂ oz) butter

40 g (1¹/₂ oz) plain flour

570 ml (1 pint) milk

a little freshly grated nutmeg

pinch of cayenne pepper

50 g (2 oz) mature Cheddar cheese, grated

25 g (1 oz) Parmesan cheese, grated

a little salt and freshly ground black pepper

125 g (4¹/₂ oz) fusilli pasta

50 g (2 oz) steamed broccoli, cut into
  small florets

Melt the butter in a saucepan, stir in the flour and
cook over a low heat for 1 minute. Gradually
whisk in the milk, grated nutmeg and cayenne
pepper. Bring to the boil and whisk until you have
a smooth, glossy sauce and simmer gently for
3 minutes. Whisk in the cheese until melted and
season to taste.

Cook the pasta according to the instructions on
the packet and steam the broccoli florets until
tender. Drain the pasta and mix together with the
cheese sauce and broccoli.

Makes 2 portions

Easy cheese sauce for pasta

Gruyère and Parmesan cheese make a nice combination in this quick and
easy pasta sauce recipe. If you like you can add some steamed broccoli florets
or a little diced ham to the sauce.

25 g (1 oz) butter

25 g (1 oz) flour

300 ml (¹/₂ pint) milk

good pinch grated nutmeg

30 g (1 oz) grated Gruyère cheese

3 tbsp freshly grated Parmesan cheese

salt and white pepper

Melt the butter and stir in the flour until it forms
a smooth paste. Gradually whisk in the milk and
nutmeg, cooking over a low heat until you have
a smooth white sauce. Allow the sauce to come
to the boil and simmer for 1 minute, stirring
constantly. Take the saucepan off the heat and
stir in the cheeses until melted. Season with salt
and pepper to taste.

Makes 2 portions

Giant pasta shells with spinach and ricotta

You can also make this using cannelloni instead of pasta shells. You will need 9 cannelloni tubes, double the amount of spinach and ricotta, and you will also need to add an extra 3 tablespoons of Parmesan cheese. Cover the cannelloni with the tomato sauce and sprinkle the reserved 2 tablespoons of mozzarella and Parmesan on top. Bake in the oven at 200°C/400°/Gas Mark 6 for 25 minutes. *Suitable for freezing*

175 g (6 oz) giant pasta shells
1 tsp olive oil

TOMATO SAUCE
1 tbsp olive oil
1 small onion (approx. 75 g/3 oz), chopped
1 small clove garlic, crushed
450 g (1 lb) passata
1 tbsp tomato purée
1 tsp caster sugar

SPINACH AND RICOTTA FILLING
100 g (4 oz) fresh spinach or 40 g (1¹/₂ oz) frozen chopped spinach
125 g (4¹/₂ oz) ball mozzarella, diced
6 tbsp freshly grated Parmesan cheese
100 g (4 oz) ricotta cheese
a good pinch of nutmeg
salt and freshly ground black pepper

Cook the pasta shells for 12 minutes. Drain and run under a cold tap and toss in 1 teaspoon olive oil to prevent them sticking together.

To make the tomato sauce, heat the oil in a saucepan and fry the onion gently for 5 minutes. Add the garlic and cook for 1 minute. Add the passata, tomato purée and sugar and simmer for 5 minutes. Set aside.

If you are using fresh spinach in the filling, cook for 1¹/₂ minutes in the microwave or cook in a pan with just a little water clinging to the leaves. Drain and squeeze the liquid out with your hands and chop finely. Alternatively, use defrosted frozen chopped spinach and drain in a sieve to get rid of the excess water. Reserve 2 tablespoons of the mozzarella and Parmesan for the topping. Mix together the remaining mozzarella with the ricotta, Parmesan, nutmeg and seasoning. Stir in the chopped spinach.

Stuff each shell with one teaspoon of the filling. Arrange the shells in a lightly oiled ovenproof dish. Pour over the tomato sauce. Sprinkle over the reserved mozzarella and Parmesan. Bake in an oven pre-heated to 200°C/400°F/Gas Mark 6 for 25 minutes.

Makes 4 portions

Lovely lasagne

Lasagne is really popular and it's not difficult to make. I like to use the fresh lasagne sheets rather than the dried as they have a better taste and texture. It's a good idea to double the quantity when making lasagne so that you can pop one in the freezer. *Suitable for freezing*

1 tbsp olive oil

1 large onion, finely chopped

2 cloves garlic, crushed

500 g (1 lb 2 oz) lean minced beef

4 tbsp red wine or beef stock

2 x 400 g (14 oz) cans chopped tomatoes

1 tbsp fresh oregano or 1¹/₂ tsp dried oregano

CHEESE SAUCE

40 g (1¹/₂ oz) butter

40 g (1¹/₂ oz) plain flour

568 ml (1 pint) milk

a generous pinch of ground nutmeg

50 g (2 oz) Gruyère cheese, grated

9 sheets fresh lasagne

25 g (1 oz) Parmesan cheese, grated

To prepare the meat sauce, heat the oil and sauté the onion and garlic over a medium heat for about 5 minutes, or until softened and just starting to turn golden. Add the meat and cook, stirring occasionally, for a further 5 minutes. Stir in the wine or stock, tomatoes and oregano. Bring to the boil then reduce the heat and simmer gently, stirring occasionally, for 15 minutes.

To make the cheese sauce, melt the butter in a saucepan, stir in the flour and cook for 1 minute, stirring occasionally. Whisk in the milk gradually, bring to the boil and then stir over a medium heat until the sauce has thickened and is smooth. Stir in the nutmeg and Gruyère cheese until melted.

Pre-heat the oven to 190°C/375°F/Gas Mark 5. Spread about a third of the meat sauce over the base of a fairly deep, rectangular ovenproof dish (about 1.75 litres/3 pint capacity). Cover with 3 sheets of lasagne and top with a thin layer of the cheese sauce. Repeat the layers twice more. Finish with a layer of lasagne sheets and cover completely with the remaining cheese sauce, spreading it evenly over the edges using a palette knife. To finish, sprinkle the Parmesan cheese over the top. Bake in the oven for 35 to 40 minutes until bubbling and golden.

Makes 6 portions

Pasta twirls in a creamy Parmesan sauce with spring vegetables

Combining vegetables with pasta is a good way to encourage children to eat more vegetables. You can vary the vegetables you use in this recipe depending on what your child likes. Steaming vegetables makes a big difference to preserving the nutrients – if you steam broccoli it loses 20 per cent of its vitamin C but if you boil it, it loses 60 per cent.

200 g (7 oz) fusilli pasta

50 g (2 oz) broccoli florets

50 g (2 oz) cauliflower florets

1 tbsp light olive oil

1 medium onion, finely chopped

1 clove garlic, crushed

1/2 small yellow pepper, deseeded and cut into thin strips

150 g (5 oz) courgette, cut into matchsticks

3 medium ripe tomatoes, skinned, de-seeded and roughly chopped

125 ml (4 fl oz) vegetable stock

150 ml (5 fl oz) half-fat crème fraîche

75 g (3 oz) Parmesan cheese, grated

salt and pepper

Cook the pasta according to the packet instructions in a large pan of lightly salted boiling water. Steam the broccoli and cauliflower for 4 minutes, or until just tender. Meanwhile, heat the oil and sauté the onion and garlic for about 2 minutes. Add the yellow pepper and courgette and sauté for 4 to 5 minutes. Add the tomatoes and simmer for 1 minute. Stir in the vegetable stock and the crème fraîche, together with the Parmesan. Add the steamed broccoli and cauliflower and cook for about 1 minute. Season to taste. Toss the pasta with the sauce and serve with a little extra Parmesan, if you wish.

Makes 4 portions

SUPERFOOD TIP
Cauliflower

The cauliflower is a member of the cruciferous family and, like other members of this group – such as cabbage and broccoli – it contains phytochemicals that are thought to help protect against cancer by preventing cancer cells from multiplying. It also provides useful amounts of vitamin C and the B vitamins folate and B6.

SUPERFOOD TIP
Broccoli

Broccoli is rich in cancer-fighting phytochemicals – it also provides good amounts of vitamin C, folate and useful amounts of iron and dietary fibre.

Papardelle with broccoli and sunblush tomatoes

When I appeared on *Ready Steady Cook*, Nick Nairn made a very tasty simple pasta sauce similar to this. I chose broccoli as one of my ingredients as it is king of the healthy vegetable superstars.

2 tbsp light olive oil

1 medium red onion, peeled and finely sliced

175 g (6 oz) broccoli florets

1 vegetable stock cube dissolved in 350 ml (12 fl oz) water

60 g (2¹/₂ oz) sunblush tomatoes, chopped

4 tbsp double cream

25 g (1 oz) Parmesan cheese, grated

salt and freshly ground black pepper

150 g (5 oz) papardelle or tagliatelle

extra Parmesan for sprinkling on top

Heat the oil in a large pan and sauté the onion over a low heat for 10 minutes. Add the broccoli, vegetable stock and sunblush tomatoes. Reduce the heat and simmer for 7 to 8 minutes, stirring occasionally. Add the double cream and Parmesan and season with salt and pepper.

Meanwhile, cook the pasta in a large pan of lightly salted boiling water according to the instructions on the packet. Drain the pasta and toss with the broccoli and tomato sauce. Serve with extra freshly grated Parmesan cheese.

Makes 4 portions

Orzo with chicken and broccoli

Orzo is tiny pasta shaped like rice. If you can't find it, you could use small pasta shapes like tiny pasta shells instead.

1 chicken stock cube

125 g (4¹/₂ oz) orzo

1 tbsp olive oil

1 large shallot (e.g. banana shallot), finely chopped

1 chicken breast, cut into bite-sized pieces

85 g (3¹/₂ oz) broccoli, cut into small florets

60 ml (2¹/₄ fl oz) double cream

2 tsp lemon juice

25 g (2 oz) Parmesan cheese, grated

Put 450 ml (³/₄ pint) water in a pan and bring to the boil. Crumble a chicken stock cube into the boiling water, add the orzo and cook according to the packet instructions. Heat the oil in a wok and sauté the shallot and chicken for 2 to 3 minutes. Blanch the broccoli in boiling, lightly salted water for a couple of minutes. Drain the broccoli and add to the chicken together with the cream. Drain the orzo, reserving 2 tablespoons of the stock in which it was cooked. Mix the pasta together with the chicken and broccoli and stir in the 2 tablespoons of stock, the lemon juice and the Parmesan.

Makes 4 portions

Tomatoes are rich in vitamin C and B6. Canned tomatoes are rich in the phytochemical lycopene, which helps protect against certain types of cancer. The canning process helps to break down some of the tough cell walls, which makes it easier for the body to absorb lycopene.

Spaghetti with tomato sauce

This is a really good home-made tomato sauce that has a slight kick to it.
Serve with spaghetti and freshly grated Parmesan. *Sauce suitable for freezing*

2 tbsp light olive oil

1 onion, peeled and finely chopped

1 clove garlic, crushed

$1/2$ tsp dried oregano

$1/4$ tsp dried chilli, crumbled

2 x 400 g (14 oz) cans tomatoes

1 tsp balsamic vinegar

$1/2$ tsp brown sugar

salt and freshly ground black pepper

250 g (9oz) spaghetti

2 tbsp fresh basil leaves, torn

Heat the oil in a large saucepan and sauté the onion and garlic for 3 minutes. Add the oregano and dried chilli and sauté for 3 more minutes. Add the tomatoes, balsamic vinegar, sugar and seasoning and simmer gently for 15 minutes. Meanwhile, cook the spaghetti according to the instructions on the packet. After 15 minutes, break up the tomatoes using a spoon, add the torn basil leaves and continue to cook for 2 to 3 minutes. Drain the pasta and serve with the sauce.

Makes 4 portions

Annabel's Pad Thai noodles

I absolutely love Pad Thai noodles and always eat them at my favourite restaurant, E&O in Notting Hill. If you follow the instructions below they are really easy to make and I'm sure they will be popular with everyone in the family.

You can use 200 g (7 oz) of chicken breast cut into bite-sized pieces instead of prawns, if you prefer.

200 g (7 oz) raw prawns, peeled and de-veined
3 tbsp fish sauce
200 g (7 oz) medium rice noodles
2 tbsp oil for frying
2 shallots, finely sliced
1 tbsp caster sugar
2 cloves garlic, crushed
1 tsp red chilli, finely chopped
1 leek (approx. 75 g/3 oz), thinly sliced
295 g (10 oz) bean sprouts
2 eggs, lightly beaten with a little salt
2 tbsp rice wine vinegar
2 tbsp soy sauce
75 g (3 oz) honey-roasted peanuts, finely chopped

Marinate the prawns in 2 tablespoons of fish sauce for 10 minutes. (Reserve 1 tablespoon of fish sauce for later.)

Place the noodles in a pan of boiling water and add a drop of oil, stirring gently to prevent sticking. Bring it back to the boil, turn off the heat and leave to stand for 4 minutes before draining and rinsing with cold water.

Heat the oil in a wok. Stir-fry the shallots over a medium heat for about 5 minutes, or until turning brown. Sprinkle with a generous pinch of caster sugar and stir-fry for a few more minutes until crispy, then add the garlic and chilli and cook for 1 minute. Add the leek and stir-fry for 3 minutes. Add the bean sprouts (reserving a couple of handfuls) and stir-fry for 2 minutes.

Remove the prawns from the marinade, add to the wok and cook until starting to turn pink. Push all the ingredients to the side of the wok and add the eggs. Cook for about 2 minutes until scrambled, then mix with the other ingredients.

Add the drained noodles, vinegar, 1 tablespoon of the reserved fish sauce (or more, depending on taste), soy sauce and the remaining caster sugar. Cook until the noodles are warmed through. Serve in bowls with the peanuts and the reserved raw bean sprouts sprinkled over.

Makes 6 portions

Singapore noodles

I buy pre-cooked rice noodles in a packet from the supermarket for this recipe
and they are excellent. You can add more curry paste and chilli if you like this
a little hotter.

175 g (6 oz) fine egg noodles or
** 295 g (10 oz) pre-cooked, fine noodles**
a drizzle of olive oil
2 tbsp vegetable oil
2 cloves garlic, peeled and sliced
$1/2$ tsp chopped fresh root ginger, peeled
** and grated**
5 spring onions, finely sliced
$1/2$ red chilli, deseeded and finely chopped
1 tbsp korma curry paste
100 ml (3 fl oz) coconut milk
50 ml (2 fl oz) water
100 g (4 oz) frozen peas
100 g (4 oz) peeled prawns
100 g (4 oz) cooked chicken or ham, finely
** shredded**
2 tbsp soy sauce
3 to 4 drops Thai fish sauce (optional)
squeeze of lime juice

Cook the noodles according to the packet
instructions until just tender and drizzle with
a little olive oil. Alternatively, you can use
pre-cooked noodles that can be added straight
to the wok.

Heat the vegetable oil in a wok or frying pan and
stir-fry the garlic, grated ginger, spring onions
and chilli for 30 seconds. Add the curry paste and
cook for 1 minute. Add the coconut milk, water
and peas and cook for 2 minutes. Add the prawns,
shredded chicken or ham and the cooked noodles.
Stir in the soy sauce and fish sauce and stir-fry until
heated through. Squeeze over a little lime juice.

Makes 4 portions

2

Hidden vegetable tomato sauce

This is a great way to get children to eat vegetables. There are six vegetables blended into the tomato sauce and what they can't see, they can't pick out. If you don't have butternut squash you could use sweet potato instead.

2 tbsp light olive oil

1 medium onion, peeled and finely chopped

1 clove garlic, crushed

50 g (2 oz) carrots, peeled and grated

50 g (2 oz) courgettes, grated

50 g (2 oz) butternut squash, peeled and grated

50 g (2 oz) button mushrooms, sliced

1 tbsp balsamic vinegar

500 g (1 lb 2 oz) passata

2 tbsp tomato paste

1 tsp soft brown sugar

200 ml (7 fl oz) vegetable stock

¹/₂ tsp dried oregano

1 bay leaf

a handful of torn basil leaves (optional)

salt and freshly ground black pepper

Heat the oil in a saucepan and cook the onion on a low heat for 7 to 8 minutes. Add the garlic and cook for 1 minute. Add the grated carrot, courgette, butternut squash and sliced mushrooms and cook for 4 minutes, stirring occasionally. Add the balsamic vinegar and cook for 1 minute. Add the passata, tomato paste, sugar, stock, dried oregano, bay leaf and basil (if using). Cook, uncovered, over a low heat for about 35 to 40 minutes. Remove the bay leaf, transfer to a blender and blitz until smooth. Season to taste.

Makes 4 portions

SUPERFOOD TIP
Mushrooms

Mushrooms get the thumbs up for their high mineral content, especially selenium and zinc which boost the immune system and help to fight off bugs, colds, infections and viruses. They also provide copper, which the body uses for healthy skin, bones and joints – this is why many people find relief from arthritis when they wear copper bracelets.

Caroline's turkey meatballs with spaghetti and tomato sauce

Caroline Brewester – the talented runner-up on *Masterchef 2005* – sometimes comes over to cook with me. This is one of the creations we came up with, which has become a great favourite with my family. *Sauce suitable for freezing*

TURKEY MEATBALLS

2 tbsp olive oil

2 medium onions, chopped
  (approx. 175 g/6 oz)

40 g (1¹/₂ oz) white breadcrumbs
  (approx. 2 slices)

50 ml (2 fl oz) milk

250 g (9 oz) turkey mince

1 tsp fresh thyme

¹/₂ tsp salt and freshly ground black pepper

1 tbsp flour, to dust hands

2 tbsp sunflower oil, for frying

TOMATO SAUCE

Use half the onion from above

400 g (14 oz) can chopped tomatoes

100 ml (3 fl oz) water

1 tbsp tomato purée

2 tsp sugar

¹/₄ tsp oregano

pinch dried chilli flakes

salt and freshly ground black pepper

250 g (9 oz) spaghetti

Heat the oil in a pan and fry the onions gently for about 10 minutes. Meanwhile, soak the breadcrumbs in milk for 10 minutes in a large bowl.

To make the sauce, transfer half the sautéed onion to a pan, add all the other sauce ingredients and simmer for 10 minutes. To make the meatballs, add the turkey mince, thyme, the remaining sautéed onion, salt and black pepper to the soaked breadcrumbs and mix together. Using floured hands, form teaspoons of the turkey mixture into small balls. Heat the sunflower oil in a frying pan and brown the meatballs. Transfer the meatballs to the pan of tomato sauce and simmer, uncovered, for 10 minutes.

Cook the spaghetti according to the instructions on the packet. Drain and toss with the sauce.

Makes 4 portions

SUPERFOOD TIP
Pasta

Pasta is a good source of complex carbohydrates which help to provide children with energy. Pasta has a low-to-medium GI which means it's absorbed quite slowly, helping to keep blood sugar levels stable.

3 Fishy business

Penne with tuna and tomato

The fresh and semi-dried sunblush tomatoes give this dish a lovely flavour.

200 g (7 oz) penne
2 tbsp olive oil
1 red onion, peeled and sliced
4 large ripe plum tomatoes, quartered,
  de-seeded and roughly chopped
200 g (7 oz) can tuna in oil, drained
75 g (3 oz) sunblush tomatoes, chopped
1 tsp balsamic vinegar
handful of basil leaves, torn into pieces
salt and freshly ground black pepper

Cook the penne in boiling salted water according to the packet instructions. Drain and set aside. Heat the oil in a frying pan, add the onion and cook for about 6 minutes, stirring occasionally until softened. Stir in the fresh tomatoes and cook for 2 to 3 minutes, until beginning to soften. Add the tuna, sunblush tomatoes, balsamic vinegar, basil and seasoning and heat for 1 minute. Stir into the pasta and serve.

Makes 4 portions

Bow tie pasta with salmon

Pasta is very popular with children so it's a good idea to combine healthy foods like salmon or meat with pasta. You can use half-fat crème fraîche if you prefer. Make sure the tomatoes are ripe so that they have a good flavour.

125 g (4¹/₂ oz) bow tie pasta
200 g (7 oz) fresh salmon fillet, skinned
a knob of butter
salt and freshly ground black pepper
6 tbsp crème fraîche
8 tbsp tomato ketchup
1 tbsp chives, snipped
3 plum tomatoes, skinned, de-seeded
  and chopped

Cook the pasta in a large pan of lightly salted water according to the instructions on the packet. Put the salmon into a suitable microwave dish, dot with butter and season with salt and pepper. Cover and cook for 2 to 2¹/₂ minutes, according to the thickness of the fish. Strain and reserve the juices from the fish. Heat the crème fraîche, tomato ketchup and juices from the fish in a pan, stirring until blended. Add the chives and tomatoes, season to taste and simmer for 1 minute. Carefully flake the salmon, checking there are no bones, and add to the sauce. Drain the pasta and toss with the sauce.

Makes 4 portions

Honey and soy salmon kebabs

Here is a delicious, quick and easy way to cook salmon that keeps the fish really moist and tasty.

2 skinned salmon fillets, fairly thick and narrow (approx. 275 g/10 oz)

MARINADE
2 tbsp soy sauce
2 tbsp honey
1 tbsp rice wine vinegar
1 tsp vegetable oil

Mix together the ingredients for the marinade. Cut the salmon into 4 cm (1½ in) cubes and marinate in the mixture for at least 30 minutes. Meanwhile, soak four bamboo skewers in water to prevent them from getting scorched. To cook the salmon kebabs, put a little water in the base of a baking tray to prevent it becoming too hot, line it with foil and place the kebabs on the foil. Cook for 2 to 3 minutes each side under a pre-heated grill.

Makes 4 skewers

Sticky salmon

If I was asked to choose just one recipe to encourage a love of eating fish it would be this one. It's funny how the simplest recipes can often be the best.

2 skinned salmon fillets (approx. 200 g/ 7 oz), cut into 4 cm (1¹/₂ in) cubes

MARINADE
1¹/₂ tbsp soy sauce
2 tbsp ketchup
1 tbsp white wine vinegar
¹/₂ tsp sweet chilli sauce
1¹/₂ tbsp dark brown sugar

Place all the ingredients for the marinade in a small saucepan and stir over a gentle heat until the sugar has dissolved. Remove from the heat, pour into an ovenproof dish and leave to cool. Add the cubes of salmon and turn to coat them in the sauce. Leave to marinate for at least one hour.

Pre-heat the grill. Place the salmon in a baking tin lined with foil, pour over the marinade and bake for about 5 minutes, turning halfway through and basting occasionally until cooked. Remove the salmon from the baking tin and serve with easy Chinese fried rice.

Makes 4 portions

Easy Chinese fried rice

200 g (7 oz) basmati rice
65 g (2¹/₂ oz) carrots, finely chopped
75 g (3 oz) frozen peas
1 tsp vegetable oil
1 egg, lightly beaten
25 g (1 oz) butter
65 g (2¹/₄ oz) onion, finely chopped
2 tbsp soy sauce
freshly ground black pepper
1 spring onion, finely sliced

Cook the rice in a pan of lightly salted boiling water, according to the instructions on the packet, together with the chopped carrots. Four minutes before the end of the cooking time, add the frozen peas. Meanwhile, heat the vegetable oil in a frying pan or wok, beat the egg with a little salt, and pour into the pan, tilting it so that the egg coats the base. Cook until it sets as a thin omelette. Remove from the pan, roll up to form a sausage shape and cut into thin strips.

Add the butter to the wok and sauté the onion for two minutes. Add the cooked rice mixture, the soy sauce and a little freshly ground black pepper. Stir-fry the rice for about 2 minutes. Stir in the strips of egg and spring onion and heat through.

Makes 4 portions

Baked potatoes with tuna and spring onion

It's easy to pop a baking potato in the oven ready for when the children come home from school. All the following recipes are for one baked potato.

1 medium baked potato (see p. 139 for instructions on cooking baked potatoes)
$^1/_2$ x 185 g (6$^1/_2$ oz) can tuna in water, drained
2 tbsp cream cheese (approx. 25 g /1 oz)
1 spring onion, finely sliced
a few drops Tabasco to taste
25 g (1 oz) Cheddar cheese, grated

Cut the potato in half. Scoop out the flesh and mash together with the tuna, cream cheese, spring onion and Tabasco. Sprinkle the grated cheese on top and cook under a pre-heated grill for 2 to 3 minutes or until golden.

Tuna and sweetcorn topping

$^1/_2$ x 185 g (6$^1/_2$ oz) can tuna in oil, drained
1 spring onion, finely sliced
2 tbsp mayonnaise
1 tsp lime or lemon juice
2 tbsp sweetcorn

Cut the potato in half, mix all the ingredients together and divide as a topping between the baked potato halves.

Cottage cheese and prawns topping

3 tbsp cottage cheese
$^1/_2$ tsp snipped chives (or use ready-mixed cottage cheese with chives)
35 g (1$^1/_4$ oz) small cooked prawns
1 tomato, de-seeded and chopped
a little cayenne pepper or paprika

Simply mix all the ingredients together and divide between the two baked potato halves.

Prawn cocktail topping

50 g (2 oz) small cooked prawns
3 tbsp mayonnaise
pinch of sugar
1 tsp tomato ketchup
a few drops Tabasco
a few drops Worcestershire sauce
a squeeze of lemon or lime juice
a little salt and pepper

Simply mix all the ingredients together and divide between the two potato halves.

Chinese-style fish fillets

It's a shame that for many children the only fish they enjoy is fish fingers. If you try making dishes like this you may surprise yourself and find that your children are actually excited at the prospect of fish for supper. *Suitable for freezing*

SAUCE
250 ml (8 fl oz) chicken stock or fish stock
10 ml (¹/₂ fl oz) soy sauce
1 tsp sesame oil
1 tbsp sugar
1 tsp cider vinegar
1 tbsp cornflour
1 spring onion, finely sliced

3 tbsp vegetable oil
100 g (4 oz) courgette, cut into strips
50 g (2 oz) red pepper, cut into strips
salt and freshly ground black pepper
plain flour
350 g (12 oz) plaice or sole fillets, skinned
  and cut into strips about 6.5 cm
  (2¹/₂ in) long

To make the sauce, mix together the stock, soy sauce, sesame oil, sugar, vinegar and cornflour. Pour the sauce into a saucepan, bring to the boil and then simmer, stirring, for 2 to 3 minutes until thickened and smooth. Stir in the spring onion.

Heat 1 tablespoon of the vegetable oil in a pan and sauté the courgette and red pepper for 4 minutes. Season the flour and dip the fish in it to lightly coat it. Heat the remaining oil in another pan and sauté the fish for about 3 minutes each side until cooked. Add the vegetables, pour over the sauce and cook for 2 minutes.

Makes 2 portions

Annabel's paella

You can add lots of different ingredients to paella. Adding sausage is nice; either slices of ordinary, cooked sausages or chorizo, which has a smoky taste. If you use chorizo, add about 50 g (2 oz) of it with the chicken and leave out the smoked paprika and use ordinary paprika instead. *Suitable for freezing*

1 tbsp vegetable oil

1 onion, finely chopped

75 g (3 oz) red pepper (approx. $1/2$ red pepper)

1 clove garlic, crushed or finely chopped

1 chicken breast (approx. 125 g/$4^{1}/_2$ oz), cut into strips

$^1/_2$ tsp smoked paprika or ordinary paprika

200 g (7 oz) long grain rice

3 tomatoes (approx. 200 g/7 oz), de-seeded and cut into 1 cm cubes

500 ml (17$^1/_2$ fl oz) chicken stock

1 tbsp tomato purée

pinch of dried chilli flakes

$^1/_3$ tsp salt

75 g (3 oz) peeled prawns

110 g (4 oz) frozen peas

3 spring onions, finely sliced

Heat the oil in a fairly large pan and sauté the onion and red pepper for 1 minute, then lower the heat and cook, covered, for about 10 minutes or until softened. Add the garlic and cook for 1 minute. Turn the heat up to high and sauté the chicken strips for 2 to 3 minutes or until the chicken turns white. Add the smoked paprika and the rice and cook gently for 2 minutes. Add the chopped tomatoes. Mix together the stock and tomato purée and pour this over the rice. Give it a quick stir and add the chilli flakes and salt. Cover and cook over a low heat for 12 to 15 minutes or until the rice is tender (check cooking instructions on the packet).

Add the prawns and peas for the last 2 to 3 minutes. Finally, stir in the chopped spring onions.

Makes 4 portions

> SUPERFOOD TIP
> ### Red Peppers
> Red peppers contain more vitamin C than green peppers and over 10 times more betacarotene.

Easy salmon fish cakes

Seventy five per cent of Britons don't eat oily fish, which is a great shame as it provides lots of health benefits. These fish cakes are very easy to prepare and taste delicious. *Suitable for freezing*

215 g (7^1/$_2$ oz) can red salmon
2^1/$_2$ tbsp spring onion, finely chopped
2^1/$_2$ tbsp tomato ketchup
75 g (3 oz) fresh white breadcrumbs
salt and freshly ground black pepper
25 g (1 oz) plain flour
1 egg, lightly beaten
2 tbsp vegetable oil

Drain the salmon and flake, checking carefully that there are no large bones and skin. In a mixing bowl, combine the salmon, spring onion, tomato ketchup, 25 g (1 oz) of the breadcrumbs and a little salt and freshly ground black pepper. Form into four fish cakes and coat first in flour, then egg and then the remaining breadcrumbs.

Heat the oil in a frying pan and sauté the fish cakes for about 1 to 2 minutes each side or until golden.

Makes 4 fish cakes

Easy prawn pilau

You could also make this with chopped chicken instead of prawns.

1 tbsp vegetable oil
1 onion, finely chopped
1 clove garlic, crushed
2 tbsp korma curry paste
300 g (10 oz) basmati rice, rinsed and drained
700 ml (1^1/$_4$ pints) chicken stock
150 g (5 oz) frozen peas
1 small red chilli, finely sliced
150 g (5 oz) cooked peeled prawns

Heat the oil in a large pan and sauté the onion and garlic for about 2 minutes. Add the curry paste and cook for 4 minutes, stirring occasionally. Add the rice to the pan and stir to coat in the curry paste. Pour in the stock and bring to the boil. Cover the pan, turn the heat down to low and simmer for about 20 minutes or until the liquid has been absorbed and the rice is cooked. Turn off the heat, add the peas, chilli and prawns, cover the pan and leave to stand for 5 minutes.

Makes 4 portions

Glazed salmon with couscous

Lovely, moist, glazed fillets of salmon on a bed of couscous with raisins
and pine nuts.

**2 skinned salmon fillets
(approx. 140 g/5 oz each)**

HONEY AND SOY GLAZE

2 tbsp honey

2 tsp lemon juice

2 tsp soy sauce

COUSCOUS

100 g (4 oz) couscous

2 tbsp raisins

125 ml (4 fl oz) hot vegetable stock

1 tsp lemon juice

1 tsp olive oil

1 spring onion, sliced

**2 tbsp toasted pine nuts (dry-fry in a small
frying pan, stirring until lightly golden)**

a little salt and freshly ground black pepper

Pre-heat the grill. Mix together all the ingredients
for the glaze and dip the salmon into it. Grill the
bottom side of the salmon for 2 minutes. Turn
over and spoon half the remaining glaze over
that side and grill for 2 minutes. Pour over the
rest of the glaze and grill for another 2 minutes.
Check whether the fish is cooked; it may need
longer, in which case baste with the juices in the
pan and cook for a couple more minutes.

To make the couscous, put the couscous and
raisins into a bowl and pour over the boiling stock.
Cover with cling film and leave to stand for 5
minutes. Stir in the lemon juice, olive oil, spring
onion and toasted pine nuts and season with salt
and pepper.

Makes 2 portions

SUPERFOOD TIP
Pine Nuts

Pine nuts are not actually nuts, but seeds, and they are packed
with nutrients including vitamin C, iron, copper, magnesium,
zinc and phosphorus. Phosphorus is the second most abundant
mineral in the body and it works with calcium to promote
healthy bones and muscles. Most of the fat in pine nuts is
the heart-friendly monounsaturated fat.

Goujons of fish with tartare sauce

These tasty goujons of fish are fun served in a rolled-up comic lined with greaseproof paper with some oven-baked chips.

6 Jacob's Cream Crackers

25 g (1 oz) Parmesan cheese, grated

³/₄ tsp salt and black pepper

1 lightly beaten egg

2 tbsp flour

150 g (5 oz) plaice fillets, skinned and cut into goujons (you could also use fillets of sole or even strips of cod)

4 tbsp vegetable oil

TARTARE SAUCE

150 ml (5 fl oz) mayonnaise

lemon juice, to taste

1 tbsp chopped parsley

1¹/₂ tbsp capers, chopped

2 tsp chopped gherkins

1 tbsp chopped chives

Put the crackers in a plastic bag and crush them with a rolling pin. Mix together the crushed crackers, Parmesan, salt and pepper. Put the beaten egg in a shallow bowl, the flour into another and the crushed crackers in a third. Dip the fish in the flour, then in the beaten egg and finally roll it in the cracker crumbs.

Heat the oil in a frying pan and sauté over a medium high heat for about 1 minute each side. Alternatively, you could bake these in an oven pre-heated to 200°C/400°F/Gas Mark 6 for 5 minutes. Drizzle them with a little oil first.

To make the tartare sauce, simply mix all the ingredients together. Serve with the plaice goujons.

Makes 3 portions

Salmon kedgeree

'Kitchri' or kedgeree originates in Anglo-India, and was traditionally a breakfast dish.

425 ml (15 fl oz) fish stock
200 g (7 oz) salmon, cut into cubes
2 tsp medium curry paste
$1/2$ tsp salt
1 onion, chopped
$1/4$ tsp turmeric
200 g (7 oz) basmati rice, rinsed
85 g ($3^1/2$ oz) frozen peas
6 spring onions, sliced
2 eggs, hard boiled and quartered

Bring the stock to the boil, reduce to a simmer and poach the salmon for 4 to 5 minutes. Remove the salmon with a slotted spoon. Stir the curry paste and salt into the stock. Fry the onion for 10 minutes over a medium heat until golden. Add the turmeric and sauté for one minute. Put the rice into the pan with the onions. Add the stock and bring to the boil, reduce the heat, cover and simmer for 8 minutes. Add the peas and the salmon and cook for a further 2 to 3 minutes or until the rice and peas are cooked and the salmon re-heated. Remove from the heat. Stir through the spring onions and garnish with the quartered boiled eggs.

Makes 4 portions

Korma curry with prawns

You can make this with prawns, chunks of cod or a mixture of the two.

400 g (14 oz) basmati rice
1 medium onion, chopped
$1/4$ tsp turmeric
1 tsp korma curry powder
2 pinches cayenne pepper
$1^1/2$ tbsp sunflower oil
$1/4$ tsp grated ginger
1 clove garlic, crushed
400 ml (14 fl oz) can coconut milk
250 g (9 oz) raw or cooked prawns or 400 g
  (14 oz) cod, cut into $2^1/2$ cm (1 in) cubes
110 g ($4^1/2$ oz) frozen peas
a little fresh coriander (optional)

Cook the basmati rice according to the packet instructions. Cook the onion and spices in the oil over a gentle heat for 15 minutes or until the onions are soft. Add the ginger and garlic and cook for 3 minutes. Add the coconut milk. Bring to the boil and simmer for 5 minutes until it starts to thicken. Add the raw prawns and cook for 2 minutes. Add the peas and cook for a further 3 minutes until the peas and prawns are cooked through. (If using cooked prawns, simply add them with the peas and cook both for 3 minutes. If using cod chunks, cook in the sauce for 1 minute, add the peas and cook for 3 minutes more or until the fish is cooked through.) Serve with a little chopped coriander, if liked.

Makes 4 portions

Fishy business

Annabel's mini fish pie

If you want your child to grow up liking fish then you should try this delicious mini fish pie. If you make individual pies in ramekin dishes they will be just the right size for small children to enjoy. *Suitable for freezing*

MASHED POTATO

375 g (13 oz) potatoes, peeled and diced

1¹/₂ tbsp milk

25 g (1 oz) butter

salt and freshly ground black pepper

15 g (¹/₂ oz) butter

25 g (1 oz) onion, peeled and finely chopped

1 tbsp flour

75 ml (2¹/₂ fl oz) milk

50 ml (2 fl oz) vegetable stock

125 g (4¹/₂ oz) cod fillet, skinned and cubed

125 g (4¹/₂ oz) salmon fillet, skinned and cubed

1 tsp chopped fresh parsley

1 bay leaf

25 g (1 oz) frozen peas

50 g (2 oz) Cheddar cheese, grated

1 lightly beaten egg

Pre-heat the oven to 180°C/350°F/Gas Mark 4. Bring a pan of lightly salted water to the boil, add the potatoes, reduce the heat and cook for 15 to 20 minutes or until tender. Drain the potatoes and mash together with the milk and butter until smooth and season to taste.

Melt the butter in a saucepan, add the onion and sauté until softened. Add the flour and cook for 30 seconds, stirring. Gradually stir in the milk and then the stock. Bring to the boil and cook for 1 minute. Add the fish with the parsley and bay leaf. Simmer for about 3 minutes and then stir in the peas and cook for 1 minute. Remove the bay leaf and stir in the cheese until melted. Season with a little salt and pepper.

Put the fish into 2 ramekin dishes and top with the mashed potato. Brush with the lightly beaten egg. Heat through in the oven for about 15 minutes then finish off under a preheated grill for a few minutes until golden.

Makes 2 portions

Tasty salmon and spinach pie

This is my favourite recipe for fish pie. You could leave out the prawns if you prefer, and you could also make this with half salmon and half cod.

MASHED POTATO

750 g (26¹/₂ oz) potatoes, peeled and cut into chunks

30 g (1 oz) butter

2 tbsp milk

salt and freshly ground black pepper

40 g (1¹/₂ oz) butter

1 medium onion, chopped (approx. 100 g/4 oz)

40 g (1¹/₂ oz) flour

225 ml (8 fl oz) milk

200 ml (7 fl oz) fish stock

³/₄ tsp salt and a little freshly ground black pepper

2 large plum tomatoes, skinned, de-seeded and chopped (approx. 215 g/7¹/₂ oz)

250 g (9 oz) fresh spinach

400 g (14 oz) salmon fillet, skinned

100 g (4 oz) small prawns

Cook the potatoes in boiling, lightly salted water for about 20 minutes. Drain and mash together with the butter and milk and season with salt and pepper to taste.

Pre-heat the oven to 180°C/350°F/Gas Mark 4. To make the sauce, melt the butter and sauté the onion for 8 to 10 minutes. Add the flour and cook for 1 minute. Gradually add the milk to make a smooth paste, then add the stock and cook, stirring, over a low heat. Bring to the boil, then lower the heat and simmer for 2 minutes. Season with the salt and pepper. (At this stage it may taste a little salty but the salmon has no seasoning so it will balance out.) Stir the chopped tomatoes into the sauce.

Carefully wash the spinach and cook with a little water still clinging to the leaves for 2 minutes until wilted. Drain, gently squeeze out excess moisture and roughly chop. Cut the salmon into chunks and arrange in an ovenproof dish. I use a fairly deep rectangular dish measuring 27 cm x 16 cm (10¹/₂ x 6 in). Scatter over the prawns. Arrange the spinach on top. Pour over the sauce and cover with the mashed potato. Mark the top of the fish pie using a fork. Bake in the oven for about 35 minutes.

Makes 5 portions

4 Time for chicken

Chicken soup with sweetcorn

This is a delicious and nutritious soup to make with the leftovers from a roast chicken. *Suitable for freezing*

40 g (1$\frac{1}{2}$ oz) butter
1 stick celery, chopped
1 onion, chopped
150 g (5 oz) potatoes, peeled and chopped
285 g (9$\frac{1}{2}$ oz) can sweetcorn
250 ml (8 fl oz) milk
300 ml ($\frac{1}{2}$ pint) chicken stock
1 bay leaf
125 g (4$\frac{1}{2}$ oz) cooked chicken
$\frac{1}{4}$ tsp salt
freshly ground black pepper

Melt the butter in a large saucepan and cook the celery, onion and potato for 10 minutes. Reserve 3 teaspoons of the sweetcorn and stir the remainder into the other vegetables. Pour in the milk and stock and add the bay leaf. Tear the chicken into pieces, reserving 30 g (1 oz) of white chicken, and add the rest to the pan. Simmer for 15 minutes. Season with the salt and a little freshly ground black pepper.

Remove the bay leaf. Blitz well in a food processor or liquidizer. Stir in the reserved chicken and sweetcorn. Reheat the soup gently before serving.

Makes 4 portions

Thai-style chicken soup

Thai-style food tends to be very popular with children. This easy-to-prepare soup is ready in about 10 minutes and is almost a meal in itself. *Suitable for freezing*

1 tbsp light olive oil
150 g (5 oz) chopped onion
1 clove garlic, crushed
$\frac{1}{2}$ red chilli, finely chopped (approx. 1 tbsp)
1 chicken breast fillet, cut into thin strips
100 g (4 oz) broccoli
600 ml (1 pint) chicken stock
300 ml ($\frac{1}{2}$ pint) coconut milk
salt and freshly ground black pepper
150 g (5 oz) cooked rice (40 g/1$\frac{1}{2}$ oz uncooked weight)

Heat the oil in a pan and sauté the onion, garlic and chilli for 2 minutes. Add the strips of chicken and sauté for 2 more minutes. Cut the broccoli into small florets. Add the broccoli and chicken stock, bring to the boil and simmer for 4 minutes. Stir in the coconut milk and simmer for 2 minutes. Season to taste and stir in the cooked rice.

Makes 4 portions

Sweet and sour chicken

A very good sweet and sour sauce with oodles of child appeal. You can buy child-friendly chopsticks that are joined at the top, and which even very young children can use. They will have such fun using them that they will forget they are eating vegetables. Serve with egg fried rice.

75 g (3 oz) baby sweetcorn, cut into quarters

75 g (3 oz) carrots, cut into matchsticks

1 egg yolk

1¹/₂ tbsp cornflour

1 tbsp milk

2 tbsp vegetable oil

2 chicken breasts (approx. 275 g/10 oz) cut into bite-sized pieces

salt and freshly ground black pepper

2 spring onions, finely sliced

SAUCE

1 tbsp soy sauce

2 tbsp tomato ketchup

2 tbsp rice wine vinegar

2 tsp sugar

50 ml (2 fl oz) water

1 tsp cornflour

Steam the sweetcorn and carrot for about 6 minutes or until tender.

Meanwhile, whisk together the egg yolk, cornflour and milk. Heat the oil in a wok or frying pan. Season the chicken pieces, dip into the batter and sauté for 3 to 4 minutes. Add the spring onions and sauté for one minute.

Whisk together the ingredients for the sauce. Add the vegetables to the chicken in the pan. Pour over the sauce. Bring to the boil then simmer until thickened.

Makes 4 portions

Egg fried rice

150 g (5 oz) long grain rice

300 ml (1¹/₂ pint) chicken stock

1 tbsp vegetable oil

2 tbsp spring onion, finely chopped

2 eggs

1 tsp sesame oil

generous pinch of salt

Cook the rice in the stock according to the directions on the packet and drain. Heat the vegetable oil and sauté the spring onion for a couple of minutes. Add the drained, cooked rice and stir-fry for one to two minutes. Beat the eggs together with the sesame oil and a little salt. Drizzle the egg onto the rice and stir-fry for about 2 minutes, or until the eggs have set. Season the rice with salt.

Makes 4 portions

Jacques' sesame chicken fingers

Jacques and I are working together to build a brand that will stand for
healthy children's food that parents can trust. I think his principal reason
for wanting to work with me is that he gets to eat lots of yummy kids'
food in the name of research! When I gave him this recipe to try he said
it was the best chicken he had ever tasted...

2 chicken breasts
salt and freshly ground black pepper
200 ml (7 fl oz) buttermilk
1 tbsp lemon juice
1 tsp Worcestershire sauce
1 tsp soy sauce
$1/4$ tsp paprika
1 clove garlic, peeled and sliced
125 g ($4^1/_2$ oz) dried breadcrumbs or fresh
  white breadcrumbs
40 g ($11^1/_2$ oz) sesame seeds
a little vegetable oil for frying

Cut each chicken breast into 2 cm ($^1/_2$ in) strips
and season with salt and freshly ground pepper.
Combine the buttermilk, lemon juice, Worcestershire sauce, soy sauce, paprika and garlic in a bowl.
Add the chicken strips and toss to coat. Cover and
marinate for at least one hour or overnight.

Drain the chicken well. In a large bowl, toss the
breadcrumbs with the sesame seeds and some salt
and pepper. Heat the oil in a large frying pan. Roll
the chicken in the crumbs to coat and sauté until
golden and cooked through, turning occasionally.

Makes 4 portions

Teriyaki chicken skewers

This is also good made with chunks of chicken thigh rather than breast.
Darker chicken meat contains twice as much iron and zinc as the white meat.

MARINADE

1 clove garlic, crushed

**small piece ginger (approx. 1 cm/1¹/₂ in),
  peeled and grated**

2 tbsp soy sauce

1 tsp sesame oil

3 tsp runny honey

1 tbsp rice wine vinegar

2 large chicken breasts

1 heaped tbsp sesame seeds

Crush the garlic and grate the ginger. Mix all
the ingredients together for the marinade. Cut
each of the chicken breasts into 4 strips, and
place in the marinade for at least 30 minutes.
Soak four bamboo skewers in water. Thread
the chicken onto the skewers, sprinkle with the
sesame seeds and cook under a pre-heated
grill for 4 to 5 minutes each side.

Makes 4 skewers

Finger pickin' chicken balls

The grated apple adds a delicious flavour to these chicken balls and makes
them appealing to children. They are delicious hot or cold. *Suitable for freezing*

1 tbsp light olive oil

1 onion, finely chopped

50 g (2 oz) grated carrot

**1 large Granny Smith apple, peeled and
  grated**

**2 chicken breasts (approx. 350 g/12 oz),
  cut into chunks**

1 tbsp parsley

1 tsp fresh or ¹/₂ tsp dried thyme (optional)

50 g (2 oz) fresh white breadcrumbs

1 chicken stock cube, crumbled

flour for coating

vegetable oil for frying

Heat the oil in a pan and sauté half the onion
and the grated carrot for 3 minutes, stirring
occasionally. Using your hands, squeeze out a
little excess liquid from the grated apple. Mix
together the grated apple, chicken, onion and
carrot plus raw chopped onion, parsley and
thyme (if using), breadcrumbs and crumbled
stock cube and chop for a few seconds in a food
processor. Season with a little salt and pepper.

With your hands, form the mixture into 20 balls,
roll in flour and shallow fry until lightly golden
and cooked through (about 4 to 5 minutes).

Makes 20 chicken balls

Chicken satay

Chicken doesn't always have to be covered in breadcrumbs or batter
to appeal to children. They love chicken skewers. Try them with this delicious
marinade and dipping sauce for a tasty, easy-to-prepare supper.

MARINADE

1 tbsp soy sauce

1 clove garlic, crushed

1¹/₂ tbsp lemon juice

1 tbsp peanut butter

1 tbsp runny honey

4 chicken breasts

PEANUT SAUCE

1 tbsp vegetable oil

¹/₂ onion, finely chopped

¹/₂ tsp crushed dried chillies

75 ml (2¹/₂ fl oz) water

75 ml (2¹/₂ fl oz) coconut milk

**100 g (4 oz) crunchy or smooth
  peanut butter**

1 tsp soft brown sugar

Mix together all the ingredients for the marinade.
To flatten the chicken, cover with cling film and
carefully bash it with a rolling pin. Cut each
breast lengthways into 4 or 5 strips. Marinate the
chicken for between 15 and 30 minutes. Soak
8 bamboo or wooden skewers in cold water for
about 20 minutes – this stops them from burning
or charring when cooking.

To make the peanut sauce, heat the vegetable oil
in a pan and sauté the onion and the chillies for
4 minutes. Add the rest of the ingredients. Bring
to the boil, stirring, then cook for 2 minutes until
thickened.

Pre-heat the grill. Thread the chicken strips onto
the skewers and grill for about 4 minutes each
side, turning occasionally. Serve 2 skewers each
with some of the dipping sauce.

Makes 4 skewers

4

Time for chicken

Annabel's chicken dippers

Very yummy and a great favourite with my children. These are good served
with ketchup or tartare sauce.

2 chicken breasts (approx. 250 g/9 oz)

20 g ($^3/_4$ oz) Parmesan cheese, grated
20 g ($^3/_4$ oz) Cheddar cheese, grated
4 tbsp dried breadcrumbs
$^1/_2$ tsp paprika
$^1/_4$ or $^1/_2$ tsp cayenne pepper
salt and freshly ground black pepper
1 egg, lightly beaten
2 tbsp flour
6 tbsp sunflower oil for frying

Cut each chicken breast into 1 cm ($^1/_2$ in) strips.
Mix together the Parmesan, Cheddar, dried breadcrumbs, paprika, cayenne pepper, salt and pepper.

Place the egg in a shallow dish, the flour in
another and the cheesy breadcrumb mixture in a
third. Dip each chicken finger first into the flour,
then in the beaten egg and finally coat the chicken
in the breadcrumb mixture. Pour the sunflower oil
into a frying pan and fry over a medium heat in
batches, taking care not to crowd the pan. Sauté
for about 2 minutes each side until golden and
then drain on absorbent kitchen paper.

Makes 4 portions

Sticky chicken drumsticks

This is a recipe that my children love. They like to eat their drumsticks
with lots of barbecue sauce mixed together with the rice.

6 chicken drumsticks

MARINADE
6 tbsp soy sauce
6 tbsp tomato ketchup
4 tbsp lemon juice
1 clove garlic, crushed
4 tsp Worcestershire sauce
1$^1/_2$ tbsp olive oil
2 tbsp soft brown sugar
a little freshly ground black pepper

Score the drumsticks a few times with a sharp
knife. Mix together all the ingredients for the
marinade and marinate the drumsticks for about
30 minutes.

Pre-heat the grill. Arrange the drumsticks in a
baking tin lined with aluminium foil and grill
for 8 to 10 minutes on each side. Remove the
drumsticks and serve with rice.

Makes 6 portions

Couscous salad with turkey, cranberries and pecans

Like walnuts, pecans are a good source of unsaturated fatty acids and vitamin E. They also have a slightly sweeter flavour than walnuts that kids tend to prefer. If your children don't like dried cranberries, add raisins or chopped ready-to-eat apricots instead.

$^1/_2$ tbsp sunflower oil

100 g (4 oz) couscous

150 ml ($^1/_4$ pint) hot chicken stock

50 g (2 oz) diced cooked turkey

40 g (1$^1/_2$ oz) dried cranberries, cut in half

15 g ($^1/_2$ oz) pecans, chopped

DRESSING

3 tbsp olive oil

1 tbsp lemon juice

4 spring onions, finely sliced

Heat the oil in a deep frying pan and sauté the couscous for 5 minutes. Add the hot stock and leave to stand for 10 minutes, covered. Uncover and fluff up with a fork. Spread out the couscous on a baking sheet to cool down.

Transfer the couscous to a large bowl and mix together with the diced turkey, cranberries and pecans. Whisk together the oil and lemon juice and stir into the couscous together with the spring onions.

Makes 2–3 portions

Chicken satay with Chinese leaf, beansprouts and baby sweetcorn

Warm chicken satay with a crunchy salad and yummy dressing.

MARINADE

1 tbsp smooth peanut butter

1¹/₂ tbsp soy sauce

1¹/₂ tbsp honey

1 tbsp sunflower oil

black pepper

1 breast of chicken (approx. 125 g/4¹/₂ oz), cut into cubes

50 g (2 oz) baby corn, cut into strips

DRESSING

2 tbsp sesame oil

2 tbsp sunflower oil

1 tbsp soy sauce

1 tbsp rice wine vinegar

1 tsp fresh grated ginger

2 tsp honey

85 g (3¹/₂ oz) beansprouts

85 g (3¹/₂ oz) Chinese leaf cabbage, shredded

Mix together the ingredients for the marinade and marinate the chicken for about 30 minutes. Soak four bamboo skewers in water and pre-heat the grill to high. Thread the chicken onto the skewers and arrange on a baking sheet lined with aluminium foil. Grill for about 5 minutes on each side.

Steam the baby corn for 4 minutes and leave to cool. Mix together the ingredients for the dressing.

In a bowl, mix together the baby corn, beansprouts and Chinese cabbage and toss with the dressing. Remove the chicken from the skewers and scatter over the top of the salad. This is best served when the chicken is still warm.

Makes 2 portions

SUPERFOOD TIP
Peanut butter

Not a proper nut but a close relative to beans, peanuts provide fibre for a healthy stomach and digestion, calcium and magnesium for strong healthy bones and teeth, monounsaturated fat for a healthy heart, along with vitamin E and protein. Peanuts contain manganese needed to make our red blood cells that carry oxygen around the body.

Marina's sticky drumsticks

Marina is from the Phillipines – I have known her for more than 14 years
and she is a really special, warm person. She is also a wonderful cook.
We often spend hours in the kitchen cooking together and making up new
and interesting dishes which we then test out on my three teenage children
and their friends – who are always ravenous.

4 chicken drumsticks
a little salt and freshly ground black pepper

MARINADE
4 tbsp honey
2 tbsp soy sauce
$\frac{1}{2}$ Telma chicken stock cube, dissolved
 in 50 ml (2 fl oz) hot water
1 tsp sesame oil
$\frac{1}{2}$ tbsp cornflour
1 tbsp orange juice
1 clove garlic, peeled and sliced

Score the chicken with a sharp knife and season
with a little salt and pepper.

Mix together the honey, soy sauce, chicken stock
and sesame oil. Mix the cornflour with the orange
juice and stir into the soy sauce mixture. Add
the garlic. Marinate the drumsticks for about
20 minutes.

Pre-heat the grill to high. Line a baking tray with
foil. To prevent burning, I pour a little water into
the baking tray and then line it with foil. Remove
the garlic, place the drumsticks in the tray and
grill the chicken for 20 minutes (10 minutes each
side), or until cooked through.

Makes 4 drumsticks

4

Time for chicken

Turkey salad with sweetcorn and roast pepper

Grilling peppers helps to intensify the sweetness of peppers, which gives this salad a delicious sweetness that kids will love. Mixing yoghurt with mayonnaise and pesto gives a creamy dressing without too much fat. You could increase the dressing and add some cooked pasta shapes if you like. This salad is perfect for a summer evening.

100 g (4 oz) turkey or chicken breast, cut into fine strips

60 g (2^1/$_2$ oz) grilled red pepper strips (from a jar), cut into thin strips

50 g (2 oz) tinned sweetcorn

3 spring onions, finely sliced

DRESSING

2 tbsp mayonnaise

2 tbsp Greek yoghurt

1 tsp red pesto

a little salt and freshly ground black pepper

Mix together the turkey, red pepper, sweetcorn and spring onions in a bowl. Using a fork, whisk together the ingredients for the dressing and toss with the salad.

Makes 2–3 portions

Chicken teriyaki with spinach

It's very easy to make a delicious teriyaki sauce which gives pan-fried chicken a lovely golden, caramel coating. Although spinach is not as rich in iron as many people believe, it has lots of other good stuff to offer, such as vitamin C, betacarotene and B vitamins.

TERIYAKI SAUCE
2 tbsp sake (Japanese rice wine)
2 tbsp mirin (sweet rice wine)
3 tbsp soy sauce
1 tbsp sugar

2 chicken breasts
250 g (9 oz) fresh spinach
1 tbsp vegetable oil
a little butter

Mix together the sake, mirin, soy sauce and sugar to make the teriyaki sauce. Cover the chicken breasts with cling film and bash with a rolling pin to flatten a little. Marinate the chicken in the sauce for about 10 minutes.

Wash the spinach and shake dry.

Heat the oil in a frying pan, remove the chicken from the teriyaki sauce and reserve. Sauté the chicken for about 4 minutes on each side. Pour in the teriyaki sauce and continue to cook over a gentle heat for 2 to 3 minutes.

Meanwhile, cook the spinach in a large saucepan until just wilted. Melt a generous knob of butter and sauté the spinach in the butter for a minute or two. Season to taste.

Cut the chicken into strips and arrange on two plates on top of a bed of spinach. Pour over the teriyaki sauce.

Makes 2 portions

Kid's chicken curry

An all-time favourite with my family. Simple to make, but with a delicious mild, fruity curry flavour. It's great served with poppadams and fluffy white rice. *Suitable for freezing*

3 tbsp vegetable oil

2 chicken breasts, cut into chunks

1 onion, peeled and chopped

1 clove garlic, crushed

1 medium apple, peeled and thinly sliced

100 g (4 oz) baby sweetcorn, cut into quarters

1 tbsp korma curry paste

¹/₂ tbsp mango chutney

1 tbsp tomato purée

100 g (4 oz) frozen peas

150 ml (¹/₄ pint) coconut milk

1 chicken stock cube, dissolved in 150 ml (¹/₄ pint) boiling water

salt and freshly ground black pepper

Heat 1 tablespoon of the oil in a wok or frying pan and stir-fry the chicken for about 4 minutes. Remove chicken and set aside.

Heat the remaining oil in the wok and sauté the onion and garlic for 3 minutes, then add the apple and sweetcorn and stir-fry for 3 minutes.

Add the korma curry paste, mango chutney, tomato purée, frozen peas, coconut milk, chicken stock and chicken pieces and simmer for 15 to 20 minutes. Season to taste.

Makes 2 portions

SUPERFOOD TIP
Garlic

Some call it the 'stinking rose', believing it keeps vampires away and brings luck. Whatever your belief, garlic has plenty of flavour and is very healthy indeed. In fact, the Greeks and Romans ate it before going to war as they believed it made them stronger. Garlic contains vitamin C and is good for asthma sufferers. Allicin, which gives off the strong smell, helps to kill off nasty bugs, viruses and infections.

4

Time for chicken

Chicken on the griddle

Chicken is an excellent source of lean protein and provides good amounts of B vitamins and iron. Cooking chicken on a griddle pan is quick and easy and keeps the chicken tender and moist. As it requires very little fat, griddling is a good low-fat method of cooking. Chicken contains much less fat than other meats as most of the fat lies in the skin, which can be removed.

4 chicken breasts

MARINADE

1 tbsp lemon juice

1 clove garlic, crushed

2 tbsp soy sauce

2 tbsp runny honey

freshly ground black pepper

$1/2$ tbsp olive oil

a little vegetable oil

Cover the chicken breasts with cling film or greaseproof paper and flatten slightly with a mallet or a rolling pin until about $1^{1}/_{2}$ cm ($^{1}/_{2}$ in) thick.

In a bowl mix together all the ingredients for the marinade and marinate for at least one hour. Remove the chicken and reserve the marinade.

Heat the griddle (or you could use a frying pan), brush with a little oil and cook the chicken for 4 to 5 minutes on each side, or until cooked through. Strain the marinade, pour it into a small saucepan, bring to the boil and then simmer for one minute (add a little water if necessary). Serve the chicken with the sauce. If liked, serve with a selection of griddled vegetables, such as tomatoes, peppers and sweetcorn, which you can cook alongside the chicken.

Makes 4 portions

4

Time for chicken

Turkey meatloaf

A lovely moist meatloaf with hidden vegetables. Turkey is a good source of low-fat protein and provides useful amounts of B vitamins and iron – sneaking extra vegetables into dishes such as this is a good way to boost nutrient intake for children who aren't keen on their veg. *Suitable for freezing*

1 tbsp olive oil

1 large onion, finely chopped

1 clove garlic, crushed

1 medium carrot (approx. 75 g/3 oz), grated

350 g (12 oz) button mushrooms, chopped

1 tsp salt

$^1/_2$ tsp freshly ground black pepper

1$^1/_2$ tsp Worcestershire sauce

2 tbsp fresh chopped parsley

1$^1/_2$ tsp fresh thyme leaves

5 tbsp tomato ketchup

60 g (2$^1/_2$ oz) fresh white breadcrumbs (made from 2 slices white bread in a food processor)

100 ml (3 fl oz) milk

1 whole large egg and 1 large egg white, lightly beaten

550 g (1 lb 4 oz) minced turkey (mixture of light and dark meat)

Heat the oil in a large pan and sauté the onion and garlic until softened. Add the carrot and cook, stirring, for 3 minutes. Add the chopped mushrooms, half a teaspoon of salt and a quarter teaspoon of freshly ground black pepper. Cook, stirring occasionally, for about 10 minutes or until the liquid from the mushrooms has evaporated. Stir in the Worcestershire sauce, parsley, thyme and 3 tablespoons of ketchup.

In a bowl, mix the breadcrumbs together with the milk and leave to stand for 2 to 3 minutes. Stir in the beaten egg and egg white. Add the turkey, the remaining half a teaspoon of salt and quarter teaspoon of pepper. Stir until well mixed.

Spoon into a lightly oiled 23 x 13 cm (9 x 5 in) loaf tin and brush the top with the remaining 2 tablespoons of ketchup.

Bake in an oven pre-heated to 200°C/400°F/ Gas Mark 6. Serve cut into slices with some vegetables and mashed potato.

Makes 6 portions

Stir-fried rice with chicken and prawns

Fluffy basmati rice with tender chunks of marinated chicken, prawns, diced vegetables, shredded omelette and flavoured with soy sauce and spring onion.

MARINADE

1 tbsp soy sauce

1 tbsp sake

$1/4$ tsp sugar

$1/2$ tsp sesame oil

1 chicken breast, cut into small chunks

175 g (6 oz) basmati rice

4 tbsp vegetable oil

1 small onion, finely chopped

60 g ($2^1/2$ oz) red pepper, deseeded and finely chopped

salt and freshly ground black pepper to taste

1 beaten egg

60 g ($2^1/2$ oz) frozen peas

60 g ($2^1/2$ oz) frozen sweetcorn

1 large spring onion, sliced

125 g ($4^1/2$ oz) cooked prawns (optional)

1 tbsp soy sauce

Mix together the ingredients for the marinade and marinate the chicken for about 20 minutes.

Cook the rice according to the instructions on the packet. Heat half the oil in a large frying pan or wok, add the onion and sauté for 2 minutes. Add the red pepper and cook for 7 to 8 minutes.

Season the beaten egg with a little salt and pepper, pour it into the pan, tipping the pan to spread it evenly, and cook until set. Remove from the heat and break the egg up into small pieces with a wooden spatula. Return the pan to the heat, add the peas and sweetcorn and cook until tender. Remove the egg/vegetable mixture from the pan, and set aside.

Add the remaining oil and sauté the spring onion for 1 minute. Strain and reserve the marinade from the chicken and sauté the chicken for 3 to 4 minutes, or until cooked. Add the cooked rice and prawns, if using, and toss the rice over a high heat for 2 minutes.

Return the egg/vegetable mixture to the pan, add the reserved marinade, the extra tablespoon of soy sauce and toss together until heated through.

Makes 4 portions

5 Meaty goodness

Teriyaki steak

Easy, quick and delicious. Tender strips of steak on a bed of bean sprouts
with a tasty home-made teriyaki sauce. This is good served with rice.

TERIYAKI SAUCE

4 tbsp soy sauce

2 tbsp mirin (sweet Japanese rice wine)

1 tbsp sake

1 tsp sugar

2 tbsp vegetable oil

250 g (9 oz) bean sprouts

250 g (9 oz) beef fillet steak

4 spring onions, finely sliced

Combine all the ingredients together to make the
teriyaki sauce and stir to dissolve the sugar.

Heat 1 tablespoon of the oil in a non-stick frying
pan over a high heat. When hot, add the bean
sprouts and stir-fry for about one minute. Remove
and strain. Add the remaining oil to the pan.
Sear the steaks briskly over a high heat for one
minute. Turn and cook for about 2 minutes on
the other side. Remove the steaks and set aside.
Add the bean sprouts and spring onions to the
pan and stir-fry for 1 to 2 minutes, until the sauce
thickens slightly. Slice each steak into strips 2 cm
($^3/_4$ in) thick, return to the pan, toss with the
sauce and heat through.

Makes 2–3 portions

Marinated lamb kebabs

A little tzatziki would be a nice accompaniment to these kebabs.

250 g (9 oz) lamb rump steaks

MARINADE

$^1/_2$ clove garlic, crushed

1 tsp olive oil

1 tsp lemon juice

1 tsp fresh thyme leaves, chopped

Remove any fat from the lamb and cut into 2 cm
($^3/_4$ in) cubes. Put in a bowl with the marinade
ingredients. Season with pepper, but not salt.
Marinate for 1 hour or overnight in the fridge.

Soak 4 bamboo skewers in water for 30 minutes.
Season the lamb cubes with salt and thread
onto the skewers. Grill or barbecue for around
3 minutes each side and serve with a green salad
and warm pitta bread.

Makes 2 portions

Mexican beef tortillas

Wraps make trendy food for teenagers and this one is very nutritious.

MARINADE

1 tsp runny honey

1 tbsp lime juice and zest of $^1/_2$ lime

1 tbsp soy sauce

1 large shallot, finely chopped

1 clove garlic, crushed

2 tbsp olive oil

200 g (7 oz) fillet steak, tail fillet or rump steak

vegetable oil

1 ripe avocado

1$^1/_2$ tbsp lemon juice

6 tortillas

a handful of shredded cos lettuce or gem lettuce

200 g (7 oz) sour cream

Mix together the ingredients for the marinade and marinate the steaks for at least 2 hours, turning occasionally to infuse the flavours.

Brush a griddle pan with oil and heat until smoking and then add the steaks and cook for about 3 minutes on each side, depending on the thickness of the steaks. (If you don't have a griddle pan you can use a frying pan.) Remove from the pan and leave to rest for a few minutes before cutting into thin slices.

Halve, stone, peel and slice the avocado and then toss quickly in the lemon juice.

Heat the tortillas for 20 seconds in the microwave or heat for about 15 seconds each side in a dry frying pan (this makes them more pliable). Arrange some shredded lettuce in the centre, cover with the sliced avocado, beef strips and then about 2 teaspoons of the sour cream. Fold over the bottom of the tortilla, then fold in the sides and press to seal.

Makes 6 tortillas

5

Meaty goodness

SUPERFOOD TIP
Avocado

Sometimes known as the 'Alligator Pear', the avocado has a buttery texture rich in the heart-friendly monounsaturated fats that help to lower levels of LDL cholesterol. Avocados are also rich in the antioxidant lutein, which helps protect the eyes from harmful UV rays. This fruit provides fibre needed to keep the digestive and elimination system in good working order.

Evelyn's meatballs with sweet and sour sauce

My mother used to cook, but since I have been writing cookery books she has hung up her apron and prefers to come round to my house and raid my fridge instead. She and I are very close and I always value her opinion on new recipes that I create. I know when a new recipe is good because it soon goes missing!

These mini meatballs in a delicious sweet and sour sauce, served on a bed of rice, are simple to prepare and make a wonderful family meal. Serve with basmati rice. *Suitable for freezing*

MEATBALLS

450 g (1 lb) lean minced beef

1 onion, peeled and finely chopped

1 apple, peeled and grated

50 g (2 oz) fresh white breadcrumbs

1 tbsp chopped fresh parsley

1 chicken stock cube, finely crumbled

2 tbsp cold water

salt and freshly ground black pepper

2 tbsp vegetable oil for frying

SWEET AND SOUR SAUCE

1 tbsp soy sauce

1/2 tbsp cornflour

1 tbsp vegetable oil

1 onion, peeled and finely chopped

50 g (2 oz) red pepper, de-seeded and chopped

400 g (14 oz) can chopped tomatoes

1 tbsp malt vinegar

4 tbsp pineapple juice

1 tsp brown sugar

finely sliced green pepper, to garnish (optional)

Mix together all the ingredients for the meatballs and chop for a few seconds in a food processor. Using floured hands, form into about 20 meatballs. Heat the oil in a frying pan and sauté the meatballs, turning occasionally, until browned and sealed (10 to 12 minutes).

Meanwhile, to make the sauce, mix together the soy sauce and cornflour in a bowl. Heat the oil in a pan and sauté the onion for 3 minutes. Add the red pepper and sauté, stirring occasionally, for 2 minutes. Add the tomatoes, vinegar, pineapple juice and sugar, season with pepper and simmer for 10 minutes. Add the soy sauce mixture and cook for 2 minutes, stirring occasionally. Blend and sieve or purée the sauce through a mouli. Pour the sauce over the meatballs, cover and simmer or until cooked through (about 5 minutes). Garnish with finely sliced green pepper, if liked.

Makes 5 portions

Marina's tempting twirls

Minced meat in a tasty tomato sauce served with pasta twirls. Marina and I work together in the kitchen a lot experimenting and testing recipes on children. *Sauce suitable for freezing*

250 g (9 oz) fusilli pasta
2 tbsp olive oil
1 onion, finely chopped
1 clove garlic, crushed
½ red pepper, de-seeded and finely chopped
250 g (9 oz) lean minced beef
1 tbsp flatleaf parsley, finely chopped
1 tsp brown sugar
1 tsp Worcestershire sauce
1 tbsp tomato purée
2 x 400 g (14 oz) cans chopped tomatoes
1 beef stock cube dissolved in 150 ml (¼ pt)
  boiling water
4 basil leaves, torn
salt and a little freshly ground black pepper

Cook the pasta according to the instructions on the packet, drain and set aside.

Heat the olive oil in a deep saucepan and sauté the onion for about 3 minutes or until softened. Add the garlic, cook for 1 minute, then add the red pepper and cook for 5 minutes, stirring occasionally. Add the minced beef, stirring occasionally for 3 minutes, or until browned. Add the parsley, brown sugar, Worcestershire sauce, tomato purée, chopped tomatoes and beef stock, simmering for 10 minutes. Add the basil leaves and season to taste with a little salt and freshly ground black pepper. Add the cooked pasta and toss with the sauce.

Makes 4 portions

SUPERFOOD TIP
Tomatoes

Tomatoes are packed with vitamin C and the antioxidants lutein, beta-carotene and the powerful lycopene which travels around the body protecting us from cell-damaging free radicals that have been linked to heart disease and cancer. The tomato™ skin contains the highest concentration of antioxidants to protect the fruit from the sun, so this is the part that we should be eating for maximum health benefits.

Sloppy Joe with rice

This tasty minced meat dish is delicious served with rice or mashed potato.

75 g (3 oz) basmati rice
1 tbsp olive oil
1 small onion, peeled and finely chopped
1 garlic clove, peeled and crushed
100 g (4 oz) carrot, grated
250 g (8 oz) lean minced beef
400 g (14 oz) can chopped tomatoes
1 tsp red wine vinegar
1 tsp brown sugar
¹/₂ tsp salt
¹/₂ tsp Worcestershire sauce
¹/₂ tbsp tomato ketchup

Cook the rice according to the packet instructions. Meanwhile, heat the oil in a frying pan and sauté the onion, garlic and grated carrot for about 5 minutes or until softened. Add the minced beef and sauté until browned, stirring occasionally. (After it has browned, I chop the meat in a food processor for a few seconds to make it less lumpy.) Return the beef to the pan and stir in the remaining ingredients. Simmer over a low heat for about 20 minutes or until the sauce is thick. Mix with the cooked rice.

Makes 4 portions

Tender Chinese beef stir fry

You can buy pre-cooked, 'straight-to-wok' noodles in packets in the supermarket which are very good. Alternatively, cook some Chinese egg noodles or rice noodles.

250 g (9 oz) fillet or sirloin steak, cut into strips
2 tbsp cornflour
3 tbsp vegetable oil
1 onion, sliced
1 garlic clove, crushed
200 g (7 oz) broccoli, cut into small florets
1¹/₂ tbsp freshly squeezed orange juice
3 tbsp soy sauce
2 spring onions, finely sliced
250 g (9 oz) cooked noodles

Toss the beef in the cornflour and shake off any excess. Heat one tablespoon of oil in a wok or frying pan and stir-fry the beef for 2 minutes, or until golden. Remove with a slotted spoon and set aside.

Add the remaining oil to the pan and stir-fry the onion for 3 to 4 minutes. Add the garlic and cook for one minute. Blanch the broccoli in a pan of lightly salted water for 1 to 2 minutes, then drain. Add the broccoli to the beef, together with the orange juice and soy sauce, and bring to the boil. Return the beef to the pan, reduce the heat, add the spring onions and noodles and heat through.

Makes 4 portions

Nicholas's multi-layered cottage pie

A rather luxurious version of an old-fashioned, favourite comfort food.
You can either make one large cottage pie or you can make several individual
portions in ramekin dishes so that you can freeze some for use later.

My son Nicholas, who is 17, is a big meat eater and can easily eat three huge
platefuls of this for supper. *Suitable for freezing*

250 g (9 oz) swede and 200 g (7 oz) carrots,
  peeled and chopped
a generous knob of butter
2¹/₂ tbsp vegetable oil
450 g (1 lb) minced beef
1 large onion, finely chopped
100 g (4 oz) leek, finely chopped
100 g (4 oz) red pepper, finely chopped
150 g (5 oz) button mushrooms, diced
4 medium tomatoes, skinned, de-seeded
  and chopped
1 tbsp tomato purée
2 tsp Worcestershire sauce
¹/₂ tsp dried mixed herbs
1 bay leaf
1 beef stock cube dissolved in 350 ml
  (12 fl oz) boiling water
salt and freshly ground black pepper
675 g (1¹/₂ lb) potatoes, peeled and cut
  into chunks
50 g (2 oz) unsalted butter
6 tbsp milk
salt and a little white pepper
225 g (8 oz) frozen peas, cooked
1 beaten egg

Cook the swede and carrots in boiling, lightly
salted water for 20 minutes, or until tender, then
mash with the knob of butter until smooth.
Heat half a tablespoon of the oil in a large, non-
stick frying pan and sauté the minced beef for 7
to 8 minutes or until any liquid has been evaporated. Remove the beef from the pan and set
aside. Heat the remaining 2 tablespoons of oil in
a fairly large casserole and sauté the onion and
leek for 3 minutes. Add the red pepper and sauté
for 2 minutes, then add the mushrooms and garlic and sauté for 4 minutes. Add the tomatoes
and sauté for 3 minutes. Add the tomato purée,
Worcestershire sauce, herbs, bay leaf and beef
stock and simmer for about 30 minutes. Season
to taste.

Meanwhile, boil the potatoes for 15 to 20 minutes,
then drain. Return the cooked potatoes to the
empty saucepan and mash together with butter,
milk, salt and pepper until smooth.

Place the mashed carrots and swede in the base
of a glass ovenproof dish (approximately 18 cm/
7 in diameter and 7.5 cm/3 in deep). Arrange the
meat on top, then cover with a layer of cooked
peas and top with a layer of potato. Brush the
potato with the beaten egg and cook under a
pre-heated grill for 6 to 7 minutes, or until the
top is browned.

Makes 6 portions

Sesame beef stir fry

Provided you are not vegetarian, it's important to include red meat in your child's diet as red meat provides the richest source of iron, and iron deficiency is the most common nutritional deficiency in children in the UK.

This recipe is a firm family favourite in my house. I usually make it with tail fillet cut into thin strips. This is slightly cheaper than proper fillet steak but has exactly the same taste and soft texture.

1 tbsp sesame oil

1 clove garlic, crushed

1 medium carrot, cut into matchsticks

100 g (4 oz) baby sweetcorn, cut into quarters

1 courgette (approx. 100 g/4 oz), cut into matchsticks

300 g (10 oz) beef fillet or rump steak, cut into very fine strips

1 tbsp cornflour

150 ml (5 fl oz) beef stock

2 tbsp dark brown sugar

2 tbsp soy sauce

a few drops Tabasco sauce

1 tbsp sesame seeds

Heat the sesame oil in a wok and stir-fry the garlic, carrot, sweetcorn and courgette for 3 to 4 minutes. Add the beef and continue to stir-fry for 4 to 5 minutes. Mix the cornflour together with a tablespoon of water and stir into the beef stock. Stir this into the pan together with the sugar, soy sauce, Tabasco and sesame seeds. Bring to a simmer, cook until slightly thickened and serve with rice.

Makes 4 portions

SUPERFOOD TIP
Beef

Our bodies are made up of approximately 25 per cent protein and beef is a source of high-quality protein. It is also a great source of vitamin B12 which, in addition to iron, is needed to help carry oxygen around the body – and low levels can lead to lack of energy. It is also needed for healthy brain and nerve function. Additionally, beef provides the minerals selenium and zinc which may have a role to play in cancer prevention.

Annabel's Bolognese

This tasty sauce has hidden vegetables blended in, so it's great for fussy eaters.

3 tbsp vegetable oil
150 g (5 oz) onion, finely chopped
1 clove garlic
50 g (2 oz) carrot, grated
100 g (4 oz) button mushrooms, sliced
1 beef stock cube dissolved in 300 ml
 (¹/₂ pint) boiling water
250 g (9 oz) minced lean beef
300 ml (¹/₂ pint) passata
1 tbsp tomato ketchup
¹/₂ tbsp Worcestershire sauce
1 tsp brown sugar
¹/₂ tsp dried oregano
1 bay leaf
salt and freshly ground black pepper

200 g (7 oz) spaghetti

Heat half the vegetable oil in a saucepan, add half the onion and sauté for 2 minutes, stirring occasionally. Add half the crushed garlic and sauté for a few seconds. Add the carrot and mushroom and cook for 3 minutes. Transfer to a blender, stir in half the beef stock and blitz until smooth.

Meanwhile, heat the remaining oil in a saucepan, add the remaining onion and sauté for 2 minutes. Add the rest of the garlic and sauté for a few seconds. Add the minced beef and sauté, stirring occasionally for 7 to 8 minutes. Add the remaining stock, passata, tomato ketchup, Worcestershire sauce, brown sugar, oregano and bay leaf. Stir in the carrot and mushroom mixture and simmer, covered, for about 30 minutes. Remove the bay leaf. Season to taste.

Cook the spaghetti according to the instructions on the packet, drain and toss with the Bolognese sauce.

Makes 4 portions

SUPERFOOD TIP
Garlic

Containing sulphur, garlic is great for helping the liver break down and eliminate toxins from the body, especially heavy metals that we breathe in from pollution. It provides the antioxidant nutrients vitamins A and C and the mineral selenium, which all protect our cells from free radical damage. It can also help lower blood pressure and LDL cholesterol.

Smaller and sweeter than onions, shallots contain a range of minerals but have potassium and phosphorus in the greatest amounts. Phosphorus works with calcium to form strong bones and teeth and we also need it to aid contracting muscles, including those of the heart.

5

Meaty goodness

Traditional spaghetti Bolognese

2 tbsp olive oil

4 shallots, peeled and finely chopped
  (approx. 75 g/3 oz chopped weight)
  or use onion

1 clove garlic, crushed

1 medium carrot (approx. 75 g/3 oz), peeled
  and grated

450 g (1 lb) lean minced beef

1 tbsp tomato purée

150 ml (5 fl oz) beef stock

400 g (14 oz) can chopped tomatoes

1¹/₂ tsp fresh thyme leaves

a few drops Worcestershire sauce

salt and freshly ground black pepper

300 g (10 oz) spaghetti

Heat the oil in a saucepan and cook the shallots and garlic over a low heat until translucent. Add the carrot and cook for 3 minutes. Meanwhile, cook the beef in a dry frying pan, stirring occasionally for 4 minutes, breaking up with a fork until browned. Stir in the tomato purée, beef stock, chopped tomatoes, thyme, Worcestershire sauce and season with salt and pepper. Cover and cook over a low heat for about 20 minutes, stirring halfway through.

Cook the spaghetti in a large pan of lightly salted water according to the packet instructions. Drain the pasta and serve the sauce on top.

Makes 4 portions

Tasty Chinese-style minced beef

A lovely combination of minced meat with crunchy water chestnuts. Serve on its own or with rice or noodles. *Suitable for freezing*

1 tbsp sesame oil
$1/2$ small red pepper, de-seeded and cut into strips
1 onion, chopped
300 g (11 oz) minced beef
100 g (4 oz) water chestnuts, finely chopped
60 g ($2^{1}/_2$ oz) baby sweetcorn, cut into quarters
75 g (3 oz) bean sprouts
2 tbsp oyster sauce
3 tbsp rice wine vinegar

Heat the sesame oil in a wok or frying pan, add the red pepper and onion and cook for 3 minutes. Meanwhile, fry the minced meat in a dry frying pan until browned, stirring with a fork to break it up. Add the meat to the wok, stir in the water chestnuts, sweetcorn and bean sprouts and cook for 2 to 3 minutes. Stir in the oyster sauce and rice wine vinegar and stir-fry for 2 to 3 minutes, until slightly thickened.

Makes 4 portions

Indian burgers

Warm pitta pockets stuffed with lamb are delicious. If you are freezing them, separate them with waxed or greaseproof paper. *Suitable for freezing*

$1^{1}/_2$ tbsp vegetable oil
100 g (4 oz) red onion, peeled and chopped
1 tsp ground cumin
1 tsp ground coriander
$^{1}/_2$ tsp turmeric
350 g (12 oz) minced lamb
50 g (2 oz) fresh white breadcrumbs
4 tbsp beef stock
2 tbsp fresh coriander, chopped
salt and a little freshly ground black pepper
peshwari naan or pitta bread
chopped tomato and cucumber with yoghurt (optional)

Heat the oil and sauté the onion for 4 minutes, or until softened. Add the dried spices and fry gently for a few seconds. Add the minced lamb, breadcrumbs, beef stock and the fresh coriander and season to taste. Put into the food processor for a few seconds. Form into mini burgers, place them on an oiled baking sheet and grill for 5 minutes each side under a pre-heated grill. Drain on kitchen paper.

Warm the bread in the oven, or toast in a pan, and stuff with the burger. You could also add some chopped tomato, cucumber and yoghurt.

Makes 4 portions

Chilli con carne

If your children like avocado, serve this dish with a spoonful of guacamole.

75 g (3 oz) basmati rice

1 tbsp olive oil

1 small onion, peeled and finely chopped

100 g (4 oz) carrot, grated

1 garlic clove, peeled and crushed

250 g (8 oz) lean minced beef

½ tsp ground cumin

½ medium red chilli, chopped

½ tsp paprika

pinch of chilli powder or more to taste

400 g (14 oz) can chopped tomatoes

**½ beef stock cube dissolved in 50 ml
(2 fl oz) boiling water**

1 tsp red wine vinegar

1 tsp brown sugar

½ tsp dried oregano

½ tsp salt

½ tsp Worcestershire sauce

2 tbsp tomato ketchup

**295 g (10 oz) can kidney beans,
drained and dried**

Cook the rice according to the packet instructions. Heat the oil in a non-stick frying pan and sauté the onion and carrot for 5 minutes until softened. Add the garlic and cook for 1 minute. Transfer the onion and carrot mixture into a bowl and set aside. Add the minced beef to the pan and stir-fry over a high heat until browned. Add the cumin, chilli, paprika and chilli powder. Once this has cooked for 1 minute, add all the other ingredients and cook for 20 to 25 minutes.

Return the onion and carrot mixture to the pan. Simmer over a low heat for about 20 minutes or until the sauce is thick. Meanwhile cook the rice. Serve the Chilli con carne on a bed of fluffy white rice or with some mashed potato.

Makes 4 portions

SUPERFOOD TIP
Kidney Beans

Kidney beans are a double-whammy energy provider. A useful source of slow-burning complex carbohydrates and the mineral iron, which is needed for building healthy blood cells that help to energise us, they are also rich in fibre (particularly the soluble variety), which helps to keep control of cholesterol levels. They have a low GI so they help balance blood sugar levels and keep you feeling full for longer.

5

Meaty goodness

A great source of high-quality protein for growth, repair and building muscles, hormones and skin, lamb also provides the immune-boosting mineral zinc which helps build strong defences against bugs and infections. We also need zinc for our sense of taste and smell and for effective skin repair when we are injured. Lamb contains B vitamins which are needed by the body to make energy from the food that we eat.

Annabel's tasty burgers

These burgers can be made with beef, lamb or chicken. You can serve them in a toasted bun with extras like lettuce, pickled cucumber, sliced tomato, thinly sliced sautéed onion and maybe a little ketchup or mustard.

1 tbsp vegetable oil

1 onion, peeled and finely chopped

450 g (1 lb) lean minced beef or lamb

1 tbsp chopped parsley (optional)

1 beef stock cube, finely crumbled

1 apple, peeled and grated

$^1/_2$ a lightly beaten egg

60 g (2$^1/_2$ oz) fresh breadcrumbs

$^1/_2$ tbsp Worcestershire sauce

salt and freshly ground black pepper

a little flour

vegetable oil for frying, or for brushing a griddle pan

Heat the vegetable oil in a pan and fry the onion for about 5 minutes or until softened. In a mixing bowl, combine the sautéed onion together with all the other ingredients. With floured hands, form into 10 burgers.

Fry the burgers in a little hot oil in a large shallow frying pan on a high heat to brown and seal, then lower the heat and cook for 3 to 4 minutes. Turn them over and continue to cook for about 4 minutes. Alternatively, brush a griddle pan with a little oil and, when hot, place 4 burgers on the griddle and cook for about 4 minutes on each side or until browned and cooked through. Repeat with the remaining burgers.

Makes 10 burgers

Veal Milanese

This is also good made with flattened-out chicken breasts.

4 veal cutlets (each weighing approx. 100 g/4 oz)

salt and freshly ground black pepper

1 large egg

5 basil leaves, shredded (optional)

2 tbsp finely grated Parmesan cheese

100 g (4 oz) fine dried breadcrumbs

a generous knob of butter

olive oil for frying

1 lemon, cut into wedges

Flatten the veal until very thin, using a meat hammer or rolling pin, and trim away any fat. Season with a little salt and pepper. Beat the egg and add the basil and Parmesan. Pour the breadcrumbs onto a flat plate. Dip the veal into the egg and then immediately into the breadcrumbs to coat them on both sides.

Heat the butter in a large frying pan together with enough oil to cover the base of the pan. Sauté for 3 to 4 minutes on each side, until the breadcrumbs are golden and the veal cooked. You will probably need to cook these in two batches. Serve with wedges of lemon and some vegetables of your choice.

Makes 4 portions

Hungarian goulash

My mother used to make a version of this for me when I was a child and I loved it. Mine has a little bit of a kick, but you can use less cayenne pepper if you prefer. It is delicious served with noodles or rice. *Suitable for freezing*

2 tbsp flour for coating

salt and freshly ground black pepper

450 g (1 lb) lean braising steak, cut into cubes

vegetable oil for frying

2 large onions, finely sliced

1 red pepper, de-seeded and cut into strips

1/2 green pepper, de-seeded and cut into strips

1 clove garlic, crushed

2 tsp paprika

1/2 tsp cayenne pepper

2 x 400 g (14 oz) cans chopped tomatoes, drained

2 tbsp tomato purée

300 ml (10 fl oz) beef stock

2 tbsp chopped fresh parsley

3 tbsp soured cream or yoghurt

Pre-heat the oven to 150°C/300°F/Gas Mark 2. Season the flour with a little salt and pepper and roll the beef cubes in it. Fry them in the oil in 2 batches until browned on all sides. Meanwhile, sauté the onions for about 10 minutes until soft. Add the peppers and cook these for 5 minutes. Add the garlic, sprinkle over the paprika and cayenne pepper and continue to cook for about 2 minutes.

Put the meat and vegetables into a casserole dish and add all the remaining ingredients except the parsley and soured cream. Cover and cook in the oven for 1 hour 45 minutes, stirring occasionally. Finally, stir in the parsley and soured cream before serving.

Makes 6 portions

6 We love our veg

Tomato soup with pasta stars

A delicious recipe for home-made soup. You can serve this with pitta bread warmed in the oven and cut into strips, and you could serve this without the pasta if you prefer. *Suitable for freezing*

1¹/₂ tbsp olive oil

1 onion, diced

1 clove garlic, crushed

2 medium carrots (approx. 125 g/4¹/₂ oz) peeled and chopped

2 x 400 g (14 oz) cans chopped tomatoes

1 tbsp tomato purée

300 ml (¹/₂ pint) chicken or vegetable stock

1 bay leaf

sprig of fresh thyme (optional)

40 g (1¹/₂ oz) tiny pasta shapes, e.g. pasta stars

4 tbsp double cream

Heat the oil in a large saucepan and sauté the onion, garlic and carrots for 6 minutes. Stir in the tomatoes, tomato purée and stock, bay leaf and thyme (if using) and bring to a simmer. Cover with a lid and cook for 35 to 40 minutes. Meanwhile cook the pasta according to the directions on the packet.

Remove the bay leaf and the stalk from the thyme. Blitz in a food processor until smooth then stir in the double cream. Drain the pasta and stir into the soup.

Makes 8 portions

Butternut squash, carrot and ginger soup

A lovely warming soup for a cold winter's day. *Suitable for freezing*

2 tbsp olive oil

350 g (12 oz) butternut squash, peeled and diced (approx. 1 small butternut squash)

4 large carrots (300 g/10 oz), peeled and diced

2 medium onions, diced

1 large clove garlic, crushed

2 tsp ginger, grated

800 ml (28¹/₄ fl oz) vegetable stock

Heat the olive oil and cook the squash, carrots and onion over a low heat for 10 minutes. Add the garlic and ginger and cook for 1 minute. Add the stock, bring to the boil and simmer for 20 minutes.

Makes 4–5 portions

Golden lentil and vegetable soup

Sometimes it can be hard to get children to eat lentils but they are a great source
of protein and minerals. Mix them with a medley of root vegetables and you can
make a delicious soup which should go down a treat. *Suitable for freezing*

2 tbsp olive oil

1 onion, chopped

1 fat clove garlic, peeled and crushed

**2 medium carrots (approx. 110 g/4 oz),
  cut into small chunks**

**100 g (4 oz) butternut squash, peeled and
  diced**

100 g (4 oz) sweet potato, peeled and diced

200 g (7 oz) celery (2 sticks), sliced

50 ml (2 fl oz) water

100 g (4 oz) red lentils

700 ml (1¹/₄ pints) vegetable stock

1 bay leaf

1 sprig of thyme

¹/₂ tsp salt and freshly ground black pepper

Heat the oil in a fairly large pan, add the onion,
garlic and chopped vegetables. Pour over the
water and then cover and cook gently, stirring
occasionally for 15 to 20 minutes or until the
vegetables are soft. Rinse the lentils, drain and
add to the vegetables with the stock, bay leaf,
sprig of thyme and salt and pepper. Simmer for
15 minutes. Remove the bay leaf and thyme and
blitz in a food processor. Adjust the seasoning
to taste.

Makes 6 portions

6

We love our veg

SUPERFOOD TIP
Carrots

Carrots are rich in antioxidants, particularly betacarotene
which the body is able to convert into vitamin A. This is needed
to build defences against invading bacteria in the eyes, nose,
lungs and stomach. Cooked carrots have a higher concentration of antioxidants and it is especially important to eat the
skin as this is where most of the nutrients lie; the skin has to
have these to protect the carrots from UV rays and pollution.

Caramelized red onion and mozzarella wraps

These are a favourite with my son Nicholas. Wraps are fun to make and he likes arranging all the ingredients for the filling and rolling them up himself. It's interesting, I find that when children are involved in making their food they tend to enjoy eating it more.

1 tbsp olive oil

2 medium red onions, peeled and thinly sliced

1½ tsp fresh thyme, chopped

2 tsp brown sugar

2 tsp balsamic vinegar

salt and freshly ground black pepper

2 tortillas

125 g (4½ oz) ball mozzarella

20 g (¾ oz) rocket leaves (a handful)

½ tsp olive oil

a few drops balsamic vinegar

Heat the oil in a non-stick frying pan, add the onions and thyme and stir over a low heat for 15 minutes. Stir in the sugar, balsamic vinegar and seasoning and continue to cook for 5 minutes. Turn the heat up and cook for 1 minute until all the liquid has evaporated. Remove from the heat and allow to cool.

Heat the tortillas according to the packet instructions – either in a microwave or in a dry frying pan. Divide the cooked onion mixture between the tortillas, slice the mozzarella and lay on top of the onions and season. Toss the rocket leaves with the oil and balsamic vinegar and place on top of the mozzarella cheese. Roll up the tortillas and then cut in half diagonally before serving.

Makes 2 portions

SUPERFOOD TIP
Red onions

Red onions contain higher levels of a photochemical called quercetin than regular white onions. Studies suggest that quercetin helps to keep the heart healthy by preventing LDL 'bad' cholesterol from being deposited in the arteries.

Cheesy courgette sausages

If you have time, make these sausages and put them in the fridge to firm up before cooking. *Suitable for freezing before cooking*

175 g (6 oz) sliced white bread
25 g (1 oz) butter
1 medium onion, finely chopped
175 g (6 oz) courgette, grated
150 g (5 oz) Cheddar cheese, grated
1 egg, separated
a little salt and freshly ground black pepper
vegetable oil for frying

Blitz the bread in a food processor to make the breadcrumbs. Heat the butter in a frying pan and fry the onion until soft. Add the courgette and cook for 3 minutes until softened. Mix with the cheese, half the breadcrumbs, the beaten egg yolk and seasoning. Shape into 8 sausages about 10 cm (4 in) long using floured hands. Dip each sausage into the egg white, then roll in the breadcrumbs. Heat some oil in a frying pan and shallow fry the sausages until lightly golden.

Makes 8 sausages

Mini muffin pizzas

You can use whatever toppings your child likes for these mini pizzas. You can also make a simple cheese and tomato topping by arranging sliced cherry tomatoes on top of the tomato sauce and maybe some fresh basil, covering it with grated Cheddar and cooking under the grill until lightly golden.

1 English breakfast muffin, cut in half
1 tbsp tomato purée
1 tsp red pesto
1 tbsp olive oil
$^{1}/_{2}$ small red onion, peeled and sliced
2–3 button mushrooms, sliced
$^{1}/_{4}$ small courgette, thinly sliced
salt and freshly ground black pepper
60 g (2$^{1}/_{2}$ oz) mozzarella or Cheddar cheese, grated

Toast the muffin until golden and leave to cool. Pre-heat the grill to high. Mix the tomato purée and red pesto and spread over the muffins. Heat the olive oil in a frying pan and cook the onion, mushrooms and courgette until softened and golden. Add the seasoning and then divide the vegetables between the two muffin halves and top with the mozzarella or Cheddar (or a mixture of the two). Place under the grill and cook for 4 minutes or until golden and bubbling.

Makes 1 portion

Tofu and vegetable burgers

Tofu is high in protein and low in saturated fats. The combination of tofu, nuts and vegetables makes these burgers very nutritious. *Suitable for freezing*

100 g (4 oz) broccoli, cut into small florets
15 g (¹/₂ oz) butter
200 g (7 oz) button mushrooms, roughly chopped
1 clove garlic, crushed
285 g (9¹/₂ oz) packet firm tofu
100 g (4 oz) unsalted cashew nuts
3 spring onions, finely sliced
1 medium carrot, finely grated
100 g (4 oz) fresh breadcrumbs
1 tbsp oyster sauce
1 tbsp honey
salt and freshly ground black pepper
flour for coating
vegetable oil for frying

Blanch the broccoli in lightly salted boiling water until tender (2 to 3 minutes). Melt the butter in a frying pan and sauté the mushrooms and garlic until softened (about 3 to 4 minutes). Transfer to a food processor with the broccoli and all of the other burger ingredients. Process until mixed and season with salt and pepper. Form into 8 burgers, coat in flour and sauté for 2 to 3 minutes on each side over a medium heat until golden.

Makes 8 burgers

Cream cheese, spinach and tomato wrap

4 tbsp cream cheese
¹/₂ tsp red pesto
2 tortillas
4 sunblush tomatoes, chopped
a handful of baby spinach leaves

Mix together the cream cheese and red pesto. Heat the tortillas according to the instructions on the packet. Spread the tortillas with the cream cheese mixture, and cover with the chopped sunblush tomatoes and spinach leaves. Roll up and cut in half diagonally.

Makes 2 portions

Spinach salad with mango and strawberries

This is a lovely combination of flavours and is easy to prepare. In fact, I often make it as a first course when I have friends over for supper.

2 tbsp pine nuts

75 g (3 oz) baby spinach leaves

25 g (1 oz) peeled and diced red onion

1 small or $1/2$ large ripe mango, peeled and chopped

5 strawberries, hulled and sliced

2 tbsp dried cranberries

DRESSING

3 tbsp vegetable oil

1 tbsp balsamic vinegar

1 tsp caster sugar

salt and freshly ground black pepper

Heat a dry frying pan and toast the pine nuts, stirring continuously for about 2 minutes or until golden.

Meanwhile, combine all the ingredients for the salad in a bowl. Make the dressing by whisking together the oil, vinegar, sugar and seasoning. Toss the salad with the dressing and sprinkle the pine nuts over the top.

Makes 2 portions

Vegetable rösti

Instead of potato rösti, I make mine using a mixture of vegetables. You may find that even children who are not normally keen on eating vegetables will like this.

100 g (4 oz) courgette, grated

$\frac{1}{4}$ tsp salt

50 g (2 oz) sweet potato, peeled and coarsely grated

50 g (2 oz) carrots, peeled and coarsely grated

$\frac{1}{2}$ tsp fresh thyme, chopped

4 tsp plain flour

$\frac{1}{4}$ tsp salt and a little freshly ground black pepper

2 tbsp sunflower oil

Put the courgette in a colander, sprinkle over $\frac{1}{4}$ teaspoon salt and leave for 10 minutes. Squeeze any liquid out with your hands. Transfer to a bowl and mix in the sweet potato, carrot, thyme, flour and $\frac{1}{4}$ teaspoon of salt and pepper. The mixture should make a fairly thick paste.

Heat the oil in a frying pan and press heaped teaspoons of the mixture down in the pan and fry for a few minutes, turning halfway through until golden on both sides.

Makes approx. 12 mini rösti

Cheesy tomato rice

A tasty and simple-to-prepare rice dish. If you are not vegetarian you could add some diced ham with the peas.

1 onion, finely chopped

2 tbsp olive oil

1 clove garlic, crushed

2 spring onions, finely sliced

1 tbsp tomato purée

pinch of mixed herbs and pinch of sugar

150 g (5 oz) long grain rice

200 g (7 oz) canned chopped tomatoes

$\frac{1}{2}$ pint vegetable stock

75 g (3 oz) frozen peas

125 g (4$\frac{1}{2}$ oz) Cheddar cheese, grated

salt and freshly ground black pepper

Sauté the onion in the oil for 3 minutes. Add the garlic and spring onions and sauté for 1 minute. Stir in the tomato purée, herbs and sugar and cook for a few seconds. Stir in the rice and coat with the mixture. Cook for 1 minute. Stir in the chopped tomatoes and add half the stock. Cook until absorbed and then add the remaining stock. Cook for about 10 minutes, stirring occasionally. Stir in the peas and cook for 3 minutes. Remove from the heat and stir in the cheese until melted. Season to taste.

Makes 4 portions

Baked risotto with tomato, courgette and Parmesan

This is a much less time-consuming way of cooking a risotto, as all the liquid is added at the beginning. The result is delicious.

2 tbsp olive oil

1 medium onion, finely chopped

1 clove garlic, crushed

1 tsp ground sea salt

185 g (6¹/₂ oz) Arborio rice

375 ml (13¹/₄ fl oz) chicken stock

400 g (14 oz) plum tomatoes, skinned and chopped, or 400 g (14 oz) can chopped tomatoes

250 g (9 oz) or 200 g (7 oz) diced courgette

60 g (2¹/₂ oz) freshly grated Parmesan

freshly ground black pepper

25 g (1 oz) butter

2 tbsp chopped fresh parsley

Pre-heat the oven to 200°C/400°F/Gas Mark 6. Heat the oil in a 3-litre capacity ovenproof dish (with a lid) over a medium heat. Sauté the onion and garlic for 5 minutes together with the teaspoon of salt until the onion is soft and translucent. Add the rice to the dish and stir for 5 minutes. Add the stock and the chopped tomatoes and bring to simmering point, stirring occasionally. Stir in the diced courgette and sprinkle with 50 g (2 oz) of the Parmesan and some black pepper and cook for 2 minutes. Cover the dish and bake the risotto for 30 minutes, or until the rice is cooked.

Stir in the butter and remaining 10 g (¹/₂ oz) of Parmesan, cover and leave for a few minutes. Scatter parsley over the top and serve. It is best to serve this straight away but if you are re-heating it, add a little extra stock.

Makes 4 portions

Baked potatoes

Baked potatoes make a healthy alternative to chips and are a good source of energy – for a speedier version you can cook them first in the microwave. Stuffed baked potatoes are particularly delicious. All the following recipes, apart from the Chilli baked beans, are for one baked potato.

Pre-heat the oven to 200°C/400°F/Gas Mark 6. Wash and prick medium-sized baking potatoes. For a crispy skin, rub the potatoes lightly with a little olive oil before baking. Bake in the oven for about 1 hour, or until tender.

Alternatively, you can cook the potatoes in a microwave. Wash and prick the potatoes and cook on high for 10 minutes, then transfer them to an oven pre-heated to 200°C/400°F/Gas Mark 6 and cook for 30 to 35 minutes or until tender.

Cheesy baked potato with butternut squash

This combination of potato and butternut squash mixed with a little cheese and mustard is one of my favourite fillings. You can also bake butternut squash in the oven which gives it a lovely caramelized flavour. Simply cut the butternut squash in half, scoop out the seeds, brush each half with melted butter, cover with foil and bake in an oven pre-heated to 180°C/350°F/Gas mark 4 for about $1^1/_2$ hours.

100 g (4 oz) butternut squash, cut into cubes
$^1/_4$ tsp Dijon mustard
10 g ($^1/_2$ oz) freshly grated Parmesan cheese
10 g ($^1/_2$ oz) butter
salt and freshly ground black pepper
20 g ($^3/_4$ oz) Cheddar, grated

Steam the butternut squash for 10 minutes or until soft. Cut a medium-sized baked potato in half, scoop out the flesh and mash together with the cooked butternut squash, mustard, Parmesan and butter. Season with salt and pepper, put the mixture back into the potato shells, cover with the grated Cheddar and grill for 5 to 6 minutes.

Makes 1 portion

SUPERFOOD TIP
Butternut Squash

Butternut squash provides a good source of betacarotene, which is essential for growth, fighting infection, healthy skin and good vision.

Broccoli and cheese topping

25 g (4¹/₂ oz) broccoli, cut into small florets

SAUCE
15 g (¹/₂ oz) butter
15 g (¹/₂ oz) plain flour
150 ml (5 fl oz) milk
¹/₂ tsp Dijon mustard
30 g (1 oz) Cheddar cheese, grated
20 g (³/₄ oz) Parmesan cheese, grated
salt and freshly ground black pepper

Steam the broccoli for 5 to 6 minutes until tender. Refresh under a cold running tap and leave to drain.

Melt the butter, stir in the flour and cook for 1 minute. Take off the heat, and gradually whisk in the milk to make a smooth sauce. Cook over a low heat, stirring until it comes to the boil, and then cook for 1 minute – it should be quite thick. Stir in the mustard, two cheeses, salt and pepper and the broccoli. Cut a cross in the top of the potato, gently squeeze and spoon the filling into the middle.

Chilli baked beans topping

150 g (5 oz) can baked beans
2 tsp Heinz chilli sauce
6 drops Tabasco, or to taste
20 g (³/₄ oz) Cheddar, grated

Mix together the baked beans, chilli sauce and Tabasco. Cut a cross in the top of two potatoes, gently squeeze and spoon the filling into the middle. Top with the grated cheese. Place under a preheated grill until golden and bubbling.

Pizza topping

2 tbsp ready-made pizza sauce
30 g (1 oz) Cheddar cheese, grated

Take a slice off the bottom of the potato so that it sits flat. Spread with the pizza sauce and cover with the grated cheese. Cook under a pre-heated grill for about 3 minutes.

Other good toppings:

- Sour cream and chives
- Cottage cheese and chives with diced double Gloucester cheese

- Sweetcorn salsa – sweetcorn, spring onion, diced red pepper and a little mayonnaise

Pasta twirls with tomato, butternut squash and carrot sauce

This is a very tasty tomato sauce and it's bursting with betacarotene, which is important for growth, preventing infection of the nose, throat and lungs, healthy skin and good night vision. You can also mix some chopped spinach with the pasta, toss it with the tomato sauce, sprinkle some grated cheese over the top and finish off by browning the top under a pre-heated grill.

1 tbsp olive oil

125 g (4¹/₂ oz) onion, chopped

75 g (3 oz) carrot, diced

85 g (3¹/₂ oz) butternut squash, peeled and diced

3 tbsp water

1 clove garlic, finely chopped

¹/₄ tsp fresh thyme leaves

400 g (14 oz) can chopped tomatoes

1 tbsp tomato purée

100 ml (3 fl oz) water

85 g (3¹/₂ oz) Cheddar, grated

200 g (7 oz) fusilli pasta

Heat the oil in a heavy-based pan, add the onion, carrot and squash, sprinkle over the water, cover and sweat for 15 to 20 minutes or until softened.

Uncover the pan, add the garlic and thyme and cook gently for 3 minutes. Add the tomatoes, tomato purée and water and simmer for 30 minutes. Stir in the cheese until melted and purée the sauce.

Meanwhile, cook the pasta according to the packet instructions. Drain the fusilli pasta and toss with the sauce.

Makes 4 portions

SUPERFOOD TIP
Carrots

Unlike many vegetables, carrots are more nutritious when cooked because cooking breaks open the plant cells so that antioxidants and other plant chemicals can be absorbed much better. It's true that carrots do improve night vision; they are an excellent source of betacarotene which is the plant source of vitamin A and one of the first symptoms of vitamin A deficiency is night blindness.

6

We love our veg

Spaghetti primavera

You can make this with spaghetti or tagliatelle. The sauce is very simple and quick to prepare. You can use other vegetables like carrot sticks or cauliflower florets depending on what your child likes. To preserve the vitamin C content of the vegetables, cook them in the minimum amount of water until they are just tender.

150 g (5 oz) spaghetti
100 g (4 oz) broccoli, cut into small florets
75 g (3 oz) courgette, cut into strips
15 g (¹/₂ oz) butter
4 spring onions, finely sliced
100 g (4 oz) frozen peas
1 tomato (approx. 140 g/5 oz), skinned,
  de-seeded and chopped
150 ml (5 fl oz) crème fraîche
75 ml (2¹/₂ fl oz) vegetable stock
squeeze of lemon juice
4 tbsp freshly grated Parmesan cheese

Cook the spaghetti according to the instructions on the packet. Blanch the broccoli and courgette in lightly salted boiling water for 4 minutes.

Melt the butter in a saucepan and gently fry the spring onions for 1 to 2 minutes. Stir in the peas and cook for 1 minute. Stir in the chopped tomato and the blanched broccoli and courgette and cook for 1 minute more. Stir in the crème fraîche, vegetable stock, squeeze of lemon juice and Parmesan cheese. Cook over a gentle heat for 2 to 3 minutes. Season to taste then stir in the cooked spaghetti.

Makes 3 portions

7 What's for pud?

Lemon mousse with crushed meringue and raspberries

This is a fun dessert for children to make themselves.

135 g (5 oz) packet lemon jelly

150 ml (¹/₄ pint) boiling water

juice of one lemon made up to 150 ml
** (¹/₄ pint) with cold water**

250 ml (8 fl oz) double cream

300 g (10 oz) fresh raspberries

2 tbsp icing sugar

50 g (2 oz) meringue shells or nests

Cut or tear the jelly into cubes. Pour over 150 ml (¹/₄ pint) boiling water and stir until dissolved. Stir in the juice of a lemon mixed with 150 ml (¹/₄ pint) cold water. Whip the cream and stir into the jelly mixture when cool, then set aside in the fridge until this mousse just begins to set.

Purée 125 g (4¹/₂ oz) of the raspberries with the icing sugar with a hand-held electric blender and press through a sieve. Stir the remaining fresh raspberries into the raspberry sauce, reserving 8 whole fruit for decoration.

Put the meringues into a plastic bag and crush into small pieces with your fingers or a rolling pin. Take 4 knickerbocker glory glasses and divide half the broken meringue among the four glasses. Spoon over half the raspberry mixture into the four glasses and then top with half the lemon mousse divided between the glasses. Layer up with the remaining meringue and raspberry mixture, then top with the remaining lemon mousse. Finally, decorate with fresh raspberries and set aside in the fridge until ready to serve.

Makes 4 portions

Mango and strawberries with passion fruit sauce

Sometimes children's tastes can be more sophisticated than we imagine; I find that many children really like the taste of passion fruit. Passion fruit are ripe when their skin is heavily shrivelled.

2 passion fruits, halved and pulp removed

2 tbsp fresh orange juice

2 tsp honey

1 small ripe mango, peeled, stoned and cut into cubes

200 g (7 oz) strawberries, washed, hulled and quartered

Mix together the passion fruit pulp, orange juice and honey. Put the mango and strawberries in a bowl and toss with the sauce. Cover and set aside for 10 minutes before serving.

Makes 2 portions

Honey-layered yoghurt with blueberries and raspberries

This is an attractive way to serve yoghurt and fresh berries. You could use any combination of berry fruits. You could also sprinkle over a topping like granola or crushed ginger biscuits.

Blueberries

Raspberries (optional)

Natural yoghurt, e.g. Greek yoghurt

Honey or maple syrup

Mix the yoghurt with a little honey or maple syrup to sweeten. Put a layer of blueberries or a mix of blueberries and raspberries in a glass tumbler. Top with half the yoghurt mixture. Arrange another layer of berries on top and cover with the remaining yoghurt mixture.

With their high antioxidant levels, berries are some of the most delicious and powerful disease-fighting foods available. All berries are rich in vitamin C, but strawberries contain more vitamin C than any other berry fruit. The darkest coloured – blueberries, blackberries, raspberries, redcurrants and blackcurrants – contain the most protective phytochemicals. Blueberries have the highest antioxidant capacity of all fruits: the blue pigment anthocyanin helps protect us against cancer. Raspberries contain ellagic acid which can help protect against cancer.

7

What's for pud?

Simple berry fruit brulée

If you have a vanilla pod, you can split it and scrape the seeds into the cream and yoghurt mixture instead of using vanilla essence.

300 g (10 oz) mixed fresh berry fruits, e.g. blueberries, strawberries, raspberries, blackberries
150 ml (5 fl oz) double cream
150 g (5 oz) Greek yoghurt
2 tbsp icing sugar
$^1\!/_2$ tsp pure vanilla essence
$1^1\!/_2$ tbsp soft brown sugar for the topping

Pre-heat the grill to high. Divide the fresh berries between four small (10 cm/4 in diameter) ramekin dishes or heatproof glass dishes. Lightly whip the cream until it forms soft peaks. Fold in the Greek yoghurt, icing sugar and vanilla essence. Spoon the creamy yoghurt mixture over the fruits. Sprinkle over the brown sugar and cook under the grill for 2 to 3 minutes until golden and bubbling.

Makes 4 portions

Raspberry ripple dessert

You can also use this raspberry purée over vanilla ice cream, and tinned halved peaches or fresh peaches to make a peach melba.

**150 g (5 oz) raspberries, plus a few extra
  for decoration**
100 g (4 oz) icing sugar
1 tsp arrowroot, mixed with 1 tsp water
$\frac{1}{2}$ tsp freshly squeezed lemon juice
200 ml (7 fl oz) whipping cream
2 tsp icing sugar
6 drops vanilla extract
200 g (7 oz) Greek yoghurt
mint leaves (optional)
shortbread biscuits

Put the raspberries and sugar into a saucepan and cook over a low heat, stirring occasionally for 2 minutes or until mushy. Add the arrowroot paste and bring to the boil, stirring. Transfer to a bowl, add the lemon juice and set aside until cold.

Put the cream, sugar and vanilla in a bowl and whisk until just holding its shape. Whisk in half the yoghurt and, when blended, whisk in the other half. Gently fold the raspberry purée into the cream mixture, being careful not to over-mix. Spoon into 4 glasses and chill. Decorate with a few fresh raspberries and a sprig of mint, and serve with shortbread biscuits.

Makes 4 portions

What's for pud?

Apple, blackberry and pear crumble

A really good crumble bursting with fruit is comfort food at its very best. If you can't find fresh blackberries you can use frozen instead. Interestingly, frozen fruit and vegetables are often more nutritious than fresh as they are frozen within hours of being picked, thus locking in all the vital nutrients.

175 g (6 oz) plain flour

generous pinch of salt

100 g (4 oz) butter

75 g (3 oz) soft brown sugar

50 g (2 oz) ground almonds

25 g (1 oz) butter

350 g (12 oz) apples, peeled, cored and chopped

350 g (12 oz) pears, peeled, cored and chopped

finely grated zest $1/2$ lemon

50 g (2 oz) caster sugar

200 g (7 oz) blackberries

Pre-heat the oven to 200°C/400°F/Gas Mark 6. Mix the flour and salt together, and then rub the butter into the flour using your fingertips until most of the butter has been absorbed. Finally, rub in the soft brown sugar and ground almonds.

Melt the 25 g (1 oz) butter in a saucepan, add the chopped apples and pears and cook gently until just beginning to soften. Stir in the grated lemon zest, sugar and blackberries. Transfer to an ovenproof dish (a round Pyrex dish with a diameter of 17 cm/7 in and depth of 7 cm/3 in is ideal). Sprinkle over the topping and bake in the oven for 30 minutes or until golden and bubbling.

Makes 6 portions

Cranberries

Cranberries have antioxidant properties from their high tannin and vitamin C concentration. Antioxidants help protect our cells from damage caused by pollution, excess sunlight and chemicals. Cranberries are great at protecting us from bad bacteria as they contain substances that stop them setting up home in our bodies. They also support the friendly bacteria that help to keep us healthy.

Fruity cranberry and lemonade jellies

Making jelly is so easy if you use leaf gelatine – it looks a little like thin plastic sheets and dissolves into the liquid perfectly every time. If you are making this for adults you could use a sparkling wine like Prosecco instead of the lemonade and add a little more sugar to taste.

4 leaves of gelatine
290 ml (¹/₂ pint) cranberry juice
4 tbsp caster sugar
290 ml (¹/₂ pint) chilled lemonade
150 g (5 oz) mixed berry fruits,
  e.g. blueberries, raspberries and
  strawberries, hulled and quartered
creamy vanilla yoghurt (optional)

Put the gelatine leaves in a dish and cover with about 200 ml (7 fl oz) water. Follow the directions on the packet and soak the gelatine for 5 minutes.

Pour 100 ml (3 fl oz) of the cranberry juice into a saucepan, add the sugar and place over a medium heat until bubbling. Remove from the heat. Squeeze out the excess water from the gelatine leaves and stir into the warm cranberry juice until dissolved. Stir this mixture into the remaining cranberry juice. Pop in the fridge for about 10 minutes to cool down. Add the chilled lemonade and stir to mix.

Divide the fruit between 4 small glasses and pour over the jelly mixture. Place in the fridge until set. If you like you can top them with some creamy vanilla yoghurt.

Makes 4 portions

Rhubarb and strawberry crumble

Although used like a fruit, rhubarb is actually a vegetable. This is my favourite crumble recipe. *Suitable for freezing*

150 g (5 oz) plain flour

generous pinch of salt

75 g (3 oz) cold butter

85 g (3¹/₂ oz) soft brown sugar

25 g (1 oz) rolled oats

50 g (2 oz) ground almonds

350 g (12 oz) rhubarb, cut into 1 cm chunks

200 g (7 oz) strawberries, halved

75 g (3 oz) caster sugar

25 g (1 oz) ground almonds

Pre-heat the oven to 200°C/400°F/Gas Mark 6. To make the topping, mix the flour together with the salt and rub in the butter using your fingertips. When the mixture starts to stick together, add the sugar and oats and continue to rub in with your fingertips. Finally, rub in the ground almonds.

In another bowl, mix the rhubarb and strawberries together with the sugar. Sprinkle the base of a suitable ovenproof dish (a round Pyrex dish with a 17cm/7 in diameter is good) with the ground almonds. (This soaks up some of the juices from the fruits as they cook so that the crumble doesn't go soggy.) Add the fruit to the dish.

Cover the fruit with the crumble mixture and sprinkle over a little water (this helps the topping go crispy). Bake in the oven until the topping turns golden brown.

Makes 6 portions

SUPERFOOD TIP
Oats

Oats are composed mainly of complex (healthy, slow release) carbohydrates but compared to other cereals they contain higher levels of both protein and fat. They provide useful amounts of the B vitamins thiamin, riboflavin and B6 and the minerals calcium, magnesium, iron and zinc and small amounts of vitamin E, folic acid and potassium. Oats are rich in beta glucan, a type of soluble fibre that helps to reduce high blood cholesterol levels. Oats also get a big thumbs up because they have a low GI which means they are absorbed into the blood stream slowly, helping to keep blood sugar levels stable.

Ruby fruit salad

This fruit salad has a wonderful flavour due to the rose water and the pomegranates, which add a crunchy texture that complements the berry fruits. You can buy bottles of rose water in many supermarkets. This is good hot or cold and is really nice served warm with vanilla ice cream.

1 large, ripe, juicy peach

2 large, ripe, red plums

20 g (1 oz) butter

2 tbsp caster sugar

1 tbsp rose water or orange flower water

75 g (3 oz) raspberries

50 g (2 oz) redcurrants

75 g (3 oz) blackberries

1 pomegranate, cut in half and de-seeded

Halve the peach and the plums, remove the stones and cut each half into four pieces. Melt the butter in a large frying pan and place the plums and peach slices in the butter. Cook for 2 to 3 minutes before turning over and sprinkling with the sugar. Cook for a further 2 to 3 minutes and then pour over the rose water or orange flower water. Gently stir in the remaining fruits and heat through for about 1 minute.

Makes 4 portions

Amaretto and summer fruit gratin

You can make this using almost any fruits and it's good hot or cold.

2 ripe juicy peaches, skinned and cut into pieces

3 plums, skinned and cut into pieces

1 kiwi, peeled and sliced

6 strawberries, quartered

100 g (4 oz) raspberries

8 seedless grapes, cut in half

50 g (2 oz) amaretto biscuits

300 ml (¹/₂ pint) half-fat crème fraîche

2 tbsp brown sugar

Put the prepared fruit into a glass ovenproof dish. Crush the amaretto biscuits in their wrappers using a rolling pin and sprinkle the biscuits on top of the fruit. Cover with the crème fraîche. Sprinkle over the brown sugar and set aside in the fridge for at least an hour. Place under a pre-heated grill for a few minutes until golden.

Makes 4 portions

Luscious lychee frozen yoghurt

I adore frozen yoghurt and it is less rich than ice cream. Lychee is one of my favourite flavours and is very refreshing. It's worth investing in an ice cream maker – once you've tasted this you'll want to make it again and again.

500 ml (17½ fl oz) full-fat natural yoghurt
  (500 g/1 lb 2 oz pot)
150 ml (¼ pint) single cream
75 g (3 oz) caster sugar
425 g (15 oz) can lychees

Mix together the yoghurt, cream and sugar. Blend the lychees together with 200 ml (7 fl oz) of the juice from the tin. Freeze and churn the mixture in an ice cream maker. If you don't have an ice cream maker, pour the mixture into a shallow container, place in the freezer for 1 hour, then transfer to a food processor and whiz until smooth. Freeze for 2 hours, then process again before freezing until firm.

Makes 6 portions

Summer berry yoghurt ice cream

You can also make frozen yoghurt using frozen fruits.

200 g (7 oz) mixed frozen summer fruits,
  e.g. strawberries, raspberries, blackberries,
  blueberries, cherries or redcurrants
1 tbsp caster sugar
200 ml (7 fl oz) double cream
400 ml (14 fl oz) mild natural yoghurt
  (e.g. Onken set yoghurt)
75 g (3 oz) caster sugar

Put the frozen berries in a small saucepan together with 1 tablespoon of the caster sugar and cook over a gentle heat for a few minutes until soft. Purée the fruit and press through a sieve to get rid of the seeds.

Whip the cream until it forms soft peaks. Mix together the cream, yoghurt, sugar and fruit purée. Freeze in an ice cream maker or spoon into a suitable container and put in the freezer. When half-frozen (about an hour) beat it well until smooth. Return to the freezer and stir 1 or 2 more times during the remaining hour of freezing to get a smooth ice cream.

Makes 6 portions

Exotic fruit brulée

You can use any combination of fruits for this, depending on what your child likes. You can also vary the proportion of cream and yoghurt. For a lower calorie version, use more yoghurt than cream.

1 large passion fruit
1 tbsp freshly squeezed orange juice
1 tsp honey
300 g (10 oz) exotic mixed fruits, e.g. mango, kiwi or peach, peeled and chopped
150 ml (5 fl oz) double cream
100 g (4 oz) Greek yoghurt
2 tsp honey
1 heaped tbsp light muscovado sugar

Cut the passion fruit in half, scoop out the pulp and mix together with the orange juice and honey. Divide these fruits and the exotic mixed fruits between 3 small ramekin dishes approx. 9 cm (3$\frac{1}{2}$ in) in diameter. Lightly whip the cream, mix with the yoghurt and stir in the honey. Cover the fruit in the ramekins with the creamy yoghurt and honey topping, sprinkle with the sugar and place under a preheated grill for a few minutes until the sugar caramelizes.

Makes 3 portions

Caramel bananas

Caramelized banana is delicious with a toasted waffle and vanilla ice cream.

15 g ($\frac{1}{2}$ oz) butter
25 g (1 oz) soft brown sugar
2 bananas, peeled and sliced
100 ml (3 fl oz) freshly squeezed orange juice

Melt the butter in a frying pan with the brown sugar. Heat until the sugar dissolves and the butter is foaming. Add the bananas to the pan, stirring constantly. Remove from the heat and add the orange juice. Divide between two bowls and serve with a scoop of ice cream.

Makes 2 portions

SUPERFOOD TIP
Bananas

This easily digested fruit is super versatile, whether eaten alone as a snack or included in smoothies, muffins or salads. Bananas contain less water and more sugar than other soft fruits, which means they are great for providing energy. They are also packed with vitamin B6 which is needed for the production of red blood cells and for boosting the immune system that helps to keep coughs and colds at bay.

Eton mess

Indulgent and absolutely scrumptious. A fun and easy dessert for children to make themselves.

**400 g (14 oz) fresh strawberries, stalks
  removed**
4 tbsp icing sugar
200 ml (7 fl oz) double cream
65 g (2¹/₂ oz) meringue, crushed into pieces
2 passion fruits, halved

Remove the green leaves and roughly chop the strawberries. To make the strawberry purée, put half the strawberries into a small saucepan together with 2 tablespoons of icing sugar. Heat gently for about 1 minute or until softened. Whiz the strawberries in a hand blender and then push through a sieve to remove the seeds. Set aside in the fridge.

Whip the cream together with the remaining icing sugar until it forms soft peaks. Break the meringue into small pieces and fold into the whipped cream together with the remaining chopped strawberries. Cut the passion fruits in half, scoop out the flesh and add to the cream mixture. Put spoonfuls of the cream and meringue mixture into knickerbocker glory glasses, adding alternate layers of strawberry purée.

Makes 4 portions

SUPERFOOD TIP
Strawberries

Strawberries are crammed with vitamins, minerals and plant compounds, including phenols and anthocyanins that help protect the cell's DNA from damaging free radicals and offer anti-inflammatory and heart-protective properties. Strawberries are a real superfood and an excellent source of vitamin C, protecting the body from nasty bugs and infections.

Strawberry and lychee lolly

If there is one dessert that almost no child can resist it has to be an ice lolly. Unfortunately, most of the ice lollies you can buy are full of artificial colours and flavours. However, it's easy to make your own using fresh or tinned fruit, or you can make fresh fruit lollies by simply pouring fruit smoothies or pure fruit juice into special moulds. This delicious ice lolly is so simple to make and is very popular with my children.

425 g (15 oz) can lychees

150 g (5 oz) fresh strawberries, hulled and cut in half

Purée the lychees and syrup together with the fresh strawberries. Strain through a sieve. Pour into an ice lolly mould. Freeze for 2 to 3 hours or until solid.

Makes 6 lollies

Mandarin and peach ice lollies

You could also make this using peach drinking yoghurt.

400 g (14 oz) can sliced peaches in fruit juice

200 g (7 oz) pot mandarin, peach or apricot yoghurt

2 tbsp icing sugar

Drain the juice from the peaches and simply blend all the ingredients together. Pour into ice lolly moulds and freeze for about 3 hours or until solid.

Makes 8 small ice lollies

> ### SUPERFOOD TIP
> ### Yoghurt
> Many studies have shown that certain cultures in live yoghurt can help protect against infection. Some of these have been shown to keep the digestive system healthy by increasing the number of 'friendly' bacteria in the gut. Eating yoghurt after taking antibiotics is particularly important, as antibiotics kill off bad and good bacteria in the intestine and eating live yoghurt helps to restore the balance.

Although it's 92 per cent water, watermelon is crammed with powerful antioxidants. These include lycopene, which is shown to protect the body from cancer and, when combined with other nutrients, helps protect your skin from the sun, rather like an internal sunblock. Watermelon is also a good source of vitamin C, which boosts the immune system.

Watermelon cooler

300 g (10 oz) watermelon, de-seeded and cubed

75 g (3 oz) icing sugar

Blitz the watermelon together with the icing sugar and pour into lolly moulds. Freeze for 2 to 3 hours or until solid.

Makes 6 small lollies

Rhubarb and strawberry lolly

SUGAR SYRUP

100 ml (3 fl oz) boiling water

100 g (4 oz) caster sugar

100 g (4 oz) rhubarb, cut into 2 cm (1 in) chunks

150 g (5 oz) strawberries, halved

Add the boiling water to the sugar in a pan. Warm over a low heat and stir until the sugar has fully dissolved. Turn up the heat and boil for 1 minute. Add the rhubarb, turn the heat down to low and cook gently for 5 minutes. Pour the syrup and rhubarb onto the strawberries in a heatproof bowl and leave to stand for 5 minutes. Blitz in a food processor and sieve. Freeze for 2 to 3 hours or until solid.

Makes 4 lollies

Peach melba ice lolly

**250 g (9 oz) can peach slices in juice,
strained**
50 g (2 oz) fresh raspberries
100 ml (3 fl oz) raspberry drinking yoghurt
4 tsp icing sugar

Simply blend everything together. Pour into lolly
moulds and freeze for 2 to 3 hours or until solid.

Makes 8 lollies

Orange, peach and passion fruit lolly

Passion fruit has a nice flavour but can be very sour, so taste this first to
make sure the mixture is sweet enough. Remember, too, that when frozen it
will lose some of its sweetness, so do add enough sugar.

2 large passion fruit
300 ml ($^1/_2$ pint) orange juice
1 large, ripe, juicy peach
3 heaped tbsp icing sugar

Cut the passion fruit in half, scoop out the pulp
and strain the juices through a sieve. Blend
together the orange juice, peach flesh, passion
fruit juice and icing sugar. Pour into lolly moulds
and freeze for 2 to 3 hours or until solid.

Makes 8 small lollies

 More cookies and cakes please!

Chocolate fridge cake

These chocolate biscuit squares are a particular favourite of mine. You can also experiment with other combinations of biscuits, fruit and nuts; for example, you could make this using half digestive and half ginger biscuits and with dried cranberries instead of the raisins. This will keep for up to 2 weeks in the fridge. Well, maybe not…

150 g (5 oz) digestive biscuits
100 g (4 oz) milk chocolate
100 g (4 oz) plain chocolate
100 g (4 oz) golden syrup
75 g (3 oz) unsalted butter
75 g (3 oz) dried apricots, chopped
50 g (2 oz) raisins
50 g (2 oz) pecans, finely chopped
25 g (1 oz) Rice Krispies

Line a 20 cm (8 in) square shallow tin with cling film, leaving enough to hang over the sides of the tin. Break the biscuits into small pieces. Melt the two chocolates, syrup and butter in a heat-proof bowl over a pan of simmering water, stirring occasionally. Make sure that the bottom of the bowl doesn't touch the water.

Mix together the broken biscuits, chopped dried apricots, raisins, chopped pecans and Rice Krispies. Stir these into the melted chocolate mixture. Spoon the mixture into the prepared tin and level the surface by pressing down with a potato masher. Leave to cool in the tin then place in the fridge to set (which will take 1 to 2 hours). To serve, turn out, carefully peel off the cling film and cut into 12 squares.

Makes 12 portions

More cookies and cakes please!

Chewy oatmeal raisin cookies

So easy to make but these cookies are very moreish and they are good
for you, too, with oats and raisins being a good source of energy.
Suitable for freezing

115 g (4¼ oz) unsalted butter
100 g (4 oz) caster sugar
75 g (3 oz) soft brown sugar
1 egg
1 tsp pure vanilla essence
140 g (5 oz) plain flour
1 tsp baking powder
½ tsp mixed spice
½ tsp salt
100 g (4 oz) rolled oats
100 g (4 oz) raisins

Pre-heat the oven to 180°C/350°F/Gas Mark 4.
Beat the butter together with the sugars until
light and fluffy. Beat in the egg and vanilla.
Combine the flour, baking powder, mixed spice,
salt and oats and stir these into the creamed butter
and sugar mixture. Finally, stir in the raisins.

Prepare two large greased or lined baking sheets.
Form the mixture into walnut-sized balls and flatten
them with your fingers onto the baking sheets.
Space them well apart. Bake in the oven for about
15 minutes or until the edges are a light golden
brown. When the cookies are ready, leave them
to cool and then transfer them to a wire rack.
Store in a sealed container.

Makes approx. 24 cookies

SUPERFOOD TIP
Raisins

It takes 2 kg (4 lbs) of grapes to provide 450 g (1 lb) of raisins
due to the water loss that makes grapes plump and juicy.
Raisins are an excellent source of disease-fighting antioxidants
and they are also a good source of concentrated sugar.
This sugar provides energy; iron for healthy red blood cells to
carry oxygen around the body; magnesium to help the body
absorb calcium and to aid sleep; potassium for healthy nerves
and muscles; and phosphorus, which is needed to form
bones and teeth.

Chewy chocolate oatmeal cookies

Simple to make, but hard to resist! In place of chocolate chips, you can also make these cookies using white chocolate buttons, raisins or chopped dried fruit.

100 g (4 oz) butter or margarine

75 g (3 oz) brown sugar

75 g (3 oz) granulated sugar

1 egg

1 tbsp milk

1 tsp vanilla essence

100 g (4 oz) plain wholemeal flour

$1/_2$ tsp baking powder

$1/_2$ tsp bicarbonate of soda

$1/_2$ tsp salt

75 g (3 oz) rolled oats

65 g (2$1/_2$ oz) pecans, roughly chopped

100 g (4 oz) plain chocolate chips

Cream the butter or margarine with the sugars. Beat in the egg, milk and vanilla. Sift together the flour, baking powder, bicarbonate of soda and salt and beat this into the mixture. Finally stir in the oats, chopped pecans and chocolate chips.

Pre-heat the oven to 180°C/350°F/Gas Mark 4. Line 4 baking sheets with non-stick baking parchment. Form the dough into walnut-sized balls and flatten slightly onto the baking sheets, making sure they are spaced well apart. Bake for 12 to 15 minutes. They will still be quite soft but will harden once they have cooled down.

Makes approx. 20 cookies

More cookies and cakes please!

Chocolate orange mini muffins

Mini muffins are just the right size for little children and these ones are delicious.
You could also make these into regular muffins, but you will need to cook
them slightly longer.

150 g (5 oz) self-raising flour

2 tbsp cocoa powder

125 g (4¹/₂ oz) soft margarine

125 g (4¹/₂ oz) caster sugar

2 eggs, lightly beaten

75 g (3 oz) orange milk chocolate
  (e.g. Terry's), chopped into small pieces

Pre-heat the oven to 180°C/350°F/Gas Mark 4.
Sift together the flour and cocoa powder, and in
a separate bowl cream together the margarine
and caster sugar. Add the eggs to the creamed
mixture a little at a time, adding a tablespoon of
the flour mixture with the second egg. Mix in the
remaining flour and cocoa until blended. Stir in
the chocolate pieces.

Line three mini muffin trays with paper cases and
spoon in the mixture until each one is two-thirds
full. Bake in the oven for 12 to 15 minutes or until
a toothpick comes out clean (20 to 25 minutes if
making large muffins). Allow to cool for a few
minutes, then remove the muffins and place on a
wire cooling rack.

Makes 36 mini muffins or 8 large muffins

Mini blueberry muffins

When blueberries are sweet these miniature muffins are fun to make. If you don't have any mini muffin baking tins you could make these as regular-size muffins, but you will need to bake them for about 20 minutes.

75 g (3 oz) butter

200 g (7 oz) plain flour

2 tsp baking powder

100 g (4 oz) golden caster sugar

pinch of salt

1 egg

100 g (4 oz) plain yoghurt

100 ml (3 fl oz) milk

150 g (5 oz) fresh blueberries

TOPPING
25 g (1 oz) demerara sugar

Melt the butter and leave to cool. Mix all the dry ingredients in a bowl. In a separate bowl, combine the egg, yoghurt and milk with the melted butter. Pour the wet ingredients into the dry, stirring with a metal spoon (do not over-mix). Fold in the blueberries and spoon the mixture into mini muffin cases. Sprinkle the demerara sugar on top. Bake for 16 to 18 minutes at 200°C/400°F/Gas Mark 6.

Makes 28 muffins

Lara's favourite brownies

My daughter Lara is 15 and adores chocolate. She loves to make these brownies and share them with her friends. Good news for teenagers; the myth that chocolate can cause acne is not supported by any scientific evidence. These are good served warm with vanilla ice cream and hot chocolate sauce.

175 g (6 oz) unsalted butter
125 g (4¹/₂ oz) good-quality plain chocolate, broken into pieces
3 large eggs
150 g (5 oz) golden caster sugar
75 g (3 oz) ground almonds
75 g (3 oz) plain flour
50 g (2 oz) plain chocolate chips
50 g (2 oz) white chocolate, broken into pieces
icing sugar, sifted, to dust

Pre-heat the oven to 180°C/350°F/Gas Mark 4. Cut the butter into pieces, put them in a heatproof bowl with the plain chocolate and place over a pan of simmering water. Stir until melted.

Whisk the eggs and sugar together with an electric mixer for about 5 minutes or until thickened and fluffy. Stir in the melted chocolate mixture. Fold in the ground almonds, flour, plain chocolate chips and white chocolate chunks.

Grease and line a 20 cm (8 in) square tin and pour the mixture into the tin. Bake for about 30 minutes or until well risen and slightly firm at the edges. The brownie will still be soft in the centre. Leave to cool in the tin, then turn out and dust the top with sifted icing sugar. Cut into squares before serving.

These brownies are also great served as a dessert with a scoop of vanilla ice cream and hot chocolate sauce (see below).

Makes 8 brownies

Quick chocolate sauce

110 g (4 oz) plain chocolate
1 tbsp golden syrup
150 ml (¹/₄ pint) single cream

Put the chocolate, syrup and single cream in a heatproof bowl over a pan of simmering water. When the chocolate has melted, stir together and serve.

173

White chocolate and marshmallow Rice Krispie squares

Rice Krispie squares are fun and easy for children to make themselves and they are always a popular treat when friends come over after school.

100 g (4 oz) white chocolate
75 g (3 oz) unsalted butter, cut into pieces
75 g (3 oz) golden syrup
100 g (4 oz) Rice Krispies
25 g (1 oz) mini marshmallows

Break the chocolate into pieces and put into a saucepan together with the butter and golden syrup and melt over a low heat. Put the Rice Krispies into a large bowl and stir in the melted white chocolate mixture. Fold in the mini marshmallows.

Line a fairly shallow 20 cm (8 in) square baking tin. Spoon the mixture into the tin and level the surface with a potato masher. Place in the fridge to set and cut into squares before serving.

Makes 9 squares

Apricot and white chocolate Rice Krispie squares

Adding oats for long-lasting energy, nuts for protein and dried apricots for betacarotene gives these Rice Krispie squares a healthy twist.

100 g (4 oz) white chocolate
75 g (3 oz) unsalted butter
75 g (3 oz) golden syrup
60 g (2½ oz) Rice Krispies
60 g (2½ oz) porridge oats
50 g (2 oz) dried apricots, chopped
30 g (1 oz) pecans, finely chopped

Melt together the chocolate, butter and golden syrup. In a large bowl mix together the Rice Krispies, oats, dried apricots and pecans. Stir in the melted chocolate mixture.

Line a fairly shallow 20 cm (8 in) square baking tin. Spoon the mixture into the tin and level the surface with a potato masher. Place in the fridge to set and cut into squares before serving.

Makes 9 squares   *Pictured opposite*

Pierre's chocolate truffle cake

Wonderfully easy, no-cook chocolate truffle cake – more like a mousse than a cake. The first time I made this cake I invited my friend Pierre over for lunch – who likes eating almost as much as me and shares a love of chocolate. I think between the two of us we polished off the whole cake!

You could make a chocolate orange truffle cake by leaving out the coffee and adding 1½ teaspoons finely grated orange zest. For adults, add a few tablespoons of a liqueur such as Tia Maria or Kahlua. *Suitable for freezing*

250 g (9 oz) dark chocolate
2 tbsp golden syrup
2 x 284 ml ('/₂ pint) cartons double cream
4 tsp instant coffee granules
1 tsp ground cinnamon (optional)
cocoa powder for dusting

SUPERFOOD TIP
Chocolate

It's no surprise that love and chocolate go hand in hand because phenylethylamine, a naturally occuring hormone which promotes the feeling of euphoria associated with being in love, is found in chocolate. It's interesting to note that today women are the biggest buyers of chocolate, except on Valentine's Day when they hope to be receiving it.

Break the chocolate into pieces and put into a heatproof bowl together with the golden syrup and 100 ml (3 fl oz) of the cream. Place the bowl over a pan of simmering water, stirring occasionally until melted. Set aside to cool.

Line the base of an 18 cm (7 in) springform cake tin. Beat the remaining cream together with the instant coffee granules and cinnamon until the consistency of a very thick milkshake, but not quite stiff. Pour the cooled chocolate into the bowl and fold the cream and chocolate together until a solid brown colour. Pour the mixture into the prepared tin, level the surface with a palette knife or the back of a spoon. Put the tin in the fridge to firm up. It should be set in about 2 hours, or you can leave it overnight.

Unclip and remove the side of the rim. Invert a serving plate over the cake. Lift off the base and peel away the paper. Put some cocoa in a sieve and dust the surface of the cake.

Makes 12 portions

Chocolate coffee cake

This is my favourite chocolate cake recipe. Lovely and moist with a delicious chocolate flavour and it keeps really well. Instead of a coffee-flavoured butter cream filling you could make an orange butter cream by leaving out the coffee and using a tablespoon of orange juice and some grated orange zest.

You could decorate the top with sweets and novelty candles for a Birthday Cake.

130 g (4¹/₂ oz) chocolate
200 g (7 oz) plain flour
1 tsp bicarbonate of soda
170 g (6 oz) golden caster sugar
130 g (4¹/₂ oz) muscovado sugar
170 g (6 oz) softened butter
3 eggs
142 ml (4¹/₂ fl oz) carton double cream
1 tsp vanilla extract

COFFEE BUTTER CREAM
75 g (3 oz) softened butter
175 g (6 oz) icing sugar
¹/₂ tsp instant coffee dissolved in 1 tsp strong coffee.

Icing sugar for dusting

Pre-heat the oven to 180°C/ 350°F/Gas Mark 4. Grease and line 2 x 20cm (8 in) sandwich tins. Break the chocolate into pieces and melt in a heatproof bowl over a pan of simmering water and leave to cool.

Sift the flour and bicarbonate of soda into a large bowl and set aside. Beat the sugars together with the butter until smooth. Beat in the eggs one at a time. Add the chocolate and beat well. Mix the double cream with the vanilla and then add it alternately with the flour, beating after each addition. Divide the mixture between the two prepared tins, smooth the surface with a spatula and bake for about 25 minutes. Leave the cakes in their tins for a few minutes before placing them on a wire rack to cool.

To make the coffee butter cream, beat together the softened butter and icing sugar and then beat in the coffee.

Once the cakes are cool, spread the coffee icing over the top of one of the cakes and place the other cake on top. Dust with icing sugar.

Makes 8 portions

Power-packed oat bars with cranberries, apricots and pumpkin seeds

These delicious flapjack-type bars are packed full of nutritious ingredients.

80 g (3¹/₂ oz) butter

80 g (3¹/₂ oz) brown sugar

60 g (2¹/₂ oz) golden syrup

¹/₂ tsp salt

130 g (4¹/₂ oz) porridge oats

35 g (1¹/₂ oz) dried apple, chopped

35 g (1¹/₂ oz) dried apricots, chopped

25 g (1 oz) dried cranberries

25 g (1 oz) pumpkin seeds

2 tbsp sunflower seeds

25 g (1 oz) desiccated coconut

In a saucepan, melt together the butter, sugar, golden syrup and salt. Mix all the dry ingredients together in a bowl and stir in the butter and syrup mixture.

Line and grease a 20 cm (8 in) square baking tin. Spoon the mixture into the tin and press down with a potato masher to level the surface. Bake in an oven pre-heated to 180°C/350°F/Gas Mark 4 for 18 to 20 minutes. Store in the fridge and cut into bars before serving.

Makes 8 bars

Annabel's peanut butter balls

These scrummy peanut butter balls are quick and easy to make. They are a good recipe for children to prepare themselves and they taste great with or without the chocolate coating. Look out for wholenut peanut butter, which has some of the peanut skins ground up and reintroduced during the manufacturing process to increase the fibre content. Peanuts contain a range of phtyochemicals – many of which are found in the skin so wholenut peanut butter also contains higher levels of these compounds. These are believed to help protect against heart disease and certain types of cancer.

100 g (4 oz) smooth peanut butter
40 g (1¹/₂ oz) butter
40 g (1¹/₂ oz) Rice Krispies
75 g (3 oz) icing sugar
75 g (3 oz) plain chocolate, broken into pieces

Melt the peanut butter and butter in a pan over a low heat. In a bowl combine the Rice Krispies and icing sugar. Pour the peanut butter mixture into the bowl and stir with a wooden spoon until combined. Using your hands, roll into 12 small balls and put in the fridge for about 40 minutes.

These are good on their own but if you want to dip them in chocolate, melt the chocolate in a heatproof bowl over a pan of simmering water. Dip the balls halfway into the melted chocolate and then let the chocolate harden – a good way to do this is to balance the balls on an ice-cube tray.

Makes 12 balls

More cookies and cakes please!

Yummy oat and Rice Krispie squares with tropical fruits

Really simple to make – so this is a good recipe to get your children helping you in the kitchen. You can buy packets of exotic dried fruits in the supermarket.

100 g (4 oz) unsalted butter

75 g (3 oz) golden syrup

150 g (5 oz) white chocolate

100 g (4 oz) rolled oats

50 g (2 oz) Rice Krispies

125 g (4¹/₂ oz) exotic or tropical dried fruit mix, e.g. papaya, mango, melon, pineapple

Heat the butter, golden syrup and white chocolate in a large pan until melted. Stir in the oats, Rice Krispies and exotic dried fruit. Press into a 18 or 20 cm (7 or 8 in) lined tin – a potato masher is ideal for doing this. Set aside in the fridge until firm. Cut into squares before serving.

Makes 9 squares

Nir's famous chocolate cake

Nir trains at my gym and while we exercise we talk about food… Once a year everyone makes a cake and brings it in – after all, the whole point of going to the gym is so you can eat more cake! This is the chocolate cake that Nir made – it's wonderfully moist and delicious so I thought I'd share it with you.

200 g (8 oz) fine dark chocolate

200 g (8 oz) caster sugar

200 g (8 oz) butter

1 tbsp milk

4 eggs

1 tsp vanilla essence

75 g (3 oz) self-raising flour

a handful chocolate chips (optional)

icing sugar

Pre-heat the oven to 180°C/350°F/Gas Mark 4. Break the chocolate into a bowl, and add the sugar, butter and milk. Melt in the microwave or over a pan of simmering water, then stir well. Add the eggs and vanilla and whisk together. Add the flour to the mix and whisk again, then add the chocolate chips. Line a muffin tray with paper cases, pour in the mixture and bake for 10–12 minutes. Alternatively, pour into a greased 24–26 cm (9–10 in) loose-bottomed baking tin and bake for 30–35 minutes. Put a cocktail stick in the centre of the cake; if it comes out clean, it is ready. When cool, dust the top with icing sugar.

Makes 8 portions

My favourite carrot cake

This is a really delicious, moist carrot cake and you can assuage your guilt by comforting yourself that when you eat this you are getting one of your five per day portions of fruit and vegetables!

200 g (7 oz) self-raising flour

¼ tsp baking powder

¼ tsp bicarbonate of soda

a generous pinch of salt

1 tsp cinnamon

½ tsp ginger

2 large eggs, separated

250 ml (8 fl oz) sunflower oil

350 g (12 oz) soft brown sugar

½ x 225 g (8 oz) can crushed pineapple
   (150 g/5 oz drained weight)

3 medium carrots (175 g/6 oz), peeled
   and grated

75 g (3 oz) raisins (optional)

MAPLE CREAM CHEESE FROSTING

225 g (8 oz) cream cheese, at room
   temperature

100 g (4 oz) softened butter

50 g (2 oz) icing sugar

1 tbsp maple syrup

40 g (1½ oz) toasted walnuts (optional)

Line and grease a 24 cm (9 in) loose-based cake tin. Pre-heat the oven to 170°C/325°F/Gas Mark 3. Sift together the flour, baking powder, baking soda, salt, cinnamon and ginger. Whisk together the egg yolks, sunflower oil and sugar. Whisk the egg whites together with a pinch of salt in a bowl until they stand in fairly firm peaks and set aside. Mix the eggs, oil and sugar with the dry ingredients. Stir in the pineapple, carrot and raisins (if using), then gently fold in half the egg whites and then the other half. (Don't feel you have to mix the egg whites in completely.)

Pour the mixture into the prepared tin and bake for 1 to 1¼ hours or until a skewer comes out clean when inserted in the centre. Leave the cake to cool completely then remove from the tin.

To make the frosting, beat the cream cheese in a mixer until light and smooth. Remove to another bowl and then beat the butter, icing sugar and maple syrup together until fluffy and light. Fold this into the cream cheese. Spread the frosting on top of the cake using a palette knife. If you like, you can decorate the top with chopped walnuts.

Makes 10 portions

More cookies and cakes please!

Spiced pumpkin muffins

These yummy pumpkin muffins are deliciously moist and very easy to prepare. You can make them from fresh or canned pumpkin – fresh pumpkin has the best flavour.

285 g (9$^1/_2$ oz) self-raising flour

$^1/_4$ tsp bicarbonate of soda

$^1/_2$ tsp cinnamon

1$^1/_2$ tsp mixed spice

a generous pinch of salt

170 g (6 oz) soft brown sugar

30 g (1 oz) pumpkin seeds, plus 2 tbsp for sprinkling on top

100 g (4 oz) raisins

250 g (9 oz) raw pumpkin flesh, or 250 g (9 oz) canned pumpkin

150 ml (5 fl oz) sunflower oil

2 large eggs

150 ml (5 fl oz) milk

Sift together the flour, bicarbonate of soda, cinnamon, mixed spice, salt and soft brown sugar. Stir in the 30 g (1 oz) pumpkin seeds and all the raisins. If using fresh pumpkin, cut the pumpkin into chunks and steam for about 15 minutes or until tender. Purée the cooked or canned pumpkin in a blender. In a jug, whisk together the oil, eggs, milk and pumpkin purée. Add to the dry ingredients and mix quickly – don't worry if it's lumpy.

Line a muffin tray with paper cases and spoon in the mixture until about two-thirds full. Sprinkle the tops with the extra pumpkin seeds. Bake in an oven pre-heated to 180°C/350°F/Gas Mark 4 (or 160°C fan oven) for 20 to 25 minutes or until lightly golden and firm to the touch.

Makes 12 muffins

Index

A

amaretto and summer fruit
gratin 155
Annabel's Bolognese 117
Annabel's chicken dippers 94
Annabel's mini fish pie 83
Annabel's Pad Thai noodles 62
Annabel's paella 76–7
Annabel's peanut butter balls 180–1
Annabel's tasty burgers 122–3
apples 151
apple, blackberry and pear
crumble 151
and carrot muffins with maple
syrup 42–3
and raisin bran muffins 45
apricots
oat bars with 178–9
and white chocolate Rice Krispie
squares 175
autumn menu planner 14
avocado 109

B

bananas 10, 158
caramel 158
cream cheese, banana and honey
wraps 22
peach and banana smoothie 46
toasted crumpets with banana
and peanut butter 28
basil 31
beans, chilli baked beans in baked
potatoes 140
beef 116
Annabel's Bolognese 117
Annabel's tasty burgers 122–3
chilli con carne 120–1
Evelyn's meatballs with sweet and
sour sauce 110–11
Hungarian goulash 125
lovely lasagne 56
Marina's tempting twirls 112
Mexican beef tortillas 109
Nicholas's multi-layered cottage

pie 115
sesame beef stir fry 116
sloppy Joe with rice 113
tasty Chinese-style minced beef
119
tender Chinese beef stir fry 113
teriyaki steak 108
traditional spaghetti Bolognese 118
blackberries, apple, blackberry and
pear crumble 151
blood sugar levels 7, 9, 10
blueberries 172
fruity cranberry and lemonade
jellies 152–3
honey-layered yoghurt with
blueberries and raspberries 147
mini blueberry muffins 172
brain-boosting foods 8, 10
breakfasts 10, 11
broccoli
and cheese topping for baked
potatoes 140
orzo with chicken and 60
papardelle with broccoli and
sunblush tomatoes 58–9
pasta twirls with cheese sauce
and 53
brownies, Lara's favourite 173
burgers
Annabel's tasty 122–3
Indian 119
tofu and vegetable 133
butternut squash
carrot and ginger soup 128
cheesy baked potatoes with 139
pasta twirls with tomato, butternut
squash and carrot sauce 141

C

cakes
chocolate coffee cake 177
chocolate fridge 166–7
my favourite carrot cake 184
Nir's famous chocolate cake 183
Pierre's chocolate truffle 176

calcium 8
caramel bananas 158
carbohydrates 7, 9–10
Caroline's turkey meatballs with
spaghetti and tomato sauce 66–7
carrots 23, 129, 141
apple and carrot muffins with
maple syrup 42–3
butternut squash, carrot and
ginger soup 128
my favourite carrot cake 184
pasta twirls with tomato, butternut
squash and carrot sauce 141
pitta pocket with hummus and
carrot 23
cauliflower 57
cheese 26
Annabel's chicken dippers 94
in baked potato toppings 74,
138–40
baked risotto with tomato,
courgette and Parmesan 137
cheesy courgette sausages 132
cheesy muffins 26
cheesy tomato rice 136
Chef's salad 37
chopped Cobb salad 34–5
mini pitta pizzas 29
in pasta sauces 53, 54–5, 57
toasted ham and cheese muffin 25
tomato and mozzarella salad 30–1
Welsh rarebit 27
in wraps 22, 130–1, 133
Chef's salad 37
cherries 46
cherry and berry crush 46
chewy oatmeal raisin cookies 168
chicken 86–105, 102
Annabel's chicken dippers 94
Annabel's paella 76–7
chicken Caesar wrap 18
chicken wrap with tomato
pesto 19
Chinese chicken wrap 20–1
chopped Cobb salad 34–5

Index

finger pickin' chicken balls 92
on the griddle 102–3
Jacques's sesame chicken fingers
   90–1
kid's chicken curry 101
little gem cups 40
Marina's sticky drumsticks 98
orzo with chicken and broccoli 60
pasta and chicken salad with
   honey and soy
   vinaigrette 33
pasta shell salad with chicken and
   sweetcorn 32
satay 93
   with Chinese leaf, beansprouts
     and baby sweetcorn 96–7
saucy chicken gems 40
Singapore noodles 63
spaghettini with chicken, tomatoes
   and basil 50
sticky chicken drumsticks 94
stir-fried rice with chicken and
   prawns 105
sweet and sour 89
teriyaki
   chicken skewers 92
   with spinach 100
Thai-style chicken soup 88
Chinese-style fish fillets 75
chocolate 176
   apricot and white chocolate Rice
     Krispie squares 175
   coffee cake 177
   fridge cake 166–7
   Lara's favourite brownies 173
   Nir's famous chocolate cake 183
   oatmeal cookies 169
   orange mini muffins 170–1
   Pierre's chocolate truffle cake 176
   white chocolate and
     marshmallow Rice Krispie
     squares 175, 176
cod, Annabel's mini fish pie 83
coffee, chocolate coffee cake 177
constipation 7
cookies 45, 168, 169
courgettes 41
   baked risotto with tomato,
     courgette and Parmesan 137

cheesy courgette sausages 132
courgette raisin muffins 41
couscous
   glazed salmon with 79
   salad with turkey, cranberries and
     pecans 95
cranberries
   cranberry crush 46
   fruity cranberry and lemonade
     jellies 152–3
   oat bars with cranberries, apricots
     and pumpkin seeds 178–9
cream cheese, banana and honey
   wraps 22
crumble
   apple, blackberry and pear 151
   rhubarb and strawberry 154
crumpets
   crumpet pizzas 28
   toasted crumpets with banana and
     peanut butter 28

D
dairy products 8
dehydration 8, 11
dental decay 9
Dominic's hummus and ham pitta
   pockets 22
drinks
   sugar in 9
   water 8, 11

E
EFAs (Essential Fatty Acids) 8, 10
eggs 10, 11
   chopped Cobb salad 34–5
   egg fried rice 89
   Mexican egg wrap 19
   muffins with creamy scrambled
     eggs 25
   pitta pockets stuffed with tuna,
     egg and sweetcorn 24
Essential Fatty Acids (EFAs) 8, 10
Eton mess 159
Evelyn's meatballs with sweet and
   sour sauce 110–11
exams 11
exotic fruit brulée 158

F
fibre 7
fish
   oil-rich 8, 10, 70
   recipes 68–85
fruit
   amaretto and summer fruit gratin
     155
   cherry and berry crush 46
   exotic fruit brulée 158
   fruity cranberry and lemonade
     jellies 152–3
   ruby fruit salad 155
   simple berry fruit brulée 148, 149
   snacks 6
   summer berry yoghurt ice cream
     156, 157

G
garlic 101, 117
gougons of fish with tartare sauce 80
granary bread 36

H
ham
   Dominic's hummus and ham pitta
     pockets 22
   ham and pineapple pizzas 29
   little gem cups 40
   toasted ham and cheese muffin 25
hidden vegetable tomato sauce 64–5
honey-layered yoghurt with
   blueberries and raspberries 147
hummus, in pitta pockets 22, 23
Hungarian goulash 125

I
Indian burgers 119
iron deficiency 8, 10, 116

J
jellies, fruity cranberry and
   lemonade 152–3

K
kebabs
   fruit 38
   salad 38, 39
kidney beans 120

L
lamb 123
  Indian burgers 119
  marinated kebabs 108
Lara's favourite brownies 173
lasagne, lovely 56
lemon mousse with crushed
  meringue and raspberries 146
lentils, golden lentil and vegetable
  soup 129
lettuce
  fillings for lettuce leaves 40
  little gem cups 40
  saucy chicken gems 40
lollies 161–3
lovely lasagne 56
luscious lychee frozen yoghurt 156
lychees
  luscious lychee frozen yoghurt 156
  strawberry and lychee lolly 150, 151

M
mandarin and peach ice lollies
  150, 151
mangoes
  mango and strawberries with
    passion fruit sauce 147
  passion reviver 46
  spinach salad with mango and
    strawberries 134–5
Marina's tempting twirls 112
meat
  recipes 106–25
  red meat and iron 8
meatloaf, turkey 104
Mexican beef tortillas 109
Mexican egg wrap 19
muffins
  apple and carrot muffins with
    maple syrup 42–3
  apple and raisin bran 45
  cheesy 26
  chocolate orange mini 170–1
  courgette raisin 41
  with creamy scrambled eggs 25
  mini blueberry 172
  mini muffin pizzas 132
  spiced pumpkin 185
  toasted ham and cheese 25

  tuna melt 27
  Welsh rarebit 27
mushrooms 65
my favourite carrot cake 184

N
Nicholas's multi-layered cottage pie
  115
Nir's famous chocolate cake 183
noodles
  Annabel's Pad Thai 62
  Singapore 63
  tender Chinese beef stir fry 113
nutrition 6–11
  brain-boosting foods 8, 10
  carbohydrates 7, 9–10
  eggs 11
  Essential Fatty Acids (EFAs) 8, 10
  protein 7–8

O
oats 154
  bars with cranberries, apricots and
    pumpkin seeds 178–9
  cookies
    chocolate 169
    raisin 45, 168
  and Rice Krispie squares with
    tropical fruits 182, 183
oily fish 8, 10
Omega-3 fatty acids 8
orange
  chocolate orange mini muffins
    170–1
  peach and passion fruit lolly 163
orzo with chicken and broccoli 60

P
papardelle with broccoli and sunblush
  tomatoes 58–9
passion fruit
  exotic fruit brulée 158
  mango and strawberries with
    passion fruit sauce 147
  orange, peach and passion fruit
    lolly 163
  passion reviver 46
pasta 66
  recipes 48–67, 70, 112, 128

salads 30–1, 32, 33, 37, 52
  see also spaghetti
peaches
  mandarin and peach ice lollies
    150, 151
  orange, peach and passion fruit
    lolly 163
  peach and banana smoothie 46
  peach melba ice lolly 163
peanut butter 97, 180
  Annabel's peanut butter balls 180–1
pears, apple, blackberry and pear
  crumble 151
peas 50
penne with tuna and tomato 70
Pierre's chocolate truffle cake 176
pine nuts 79
pineapple 38
  ham and pineapple pizzas 29
  little gem cups 40
pitta bread
  Dominic's hummus and ham
    pockets 22
  hummus and carrot pockets 23
  mini pitta pizzas 29
  stuffed with tuna, egg and
    sweetcorn 24
pizzas
  crumpet pizzas 28
  ham and pineapple 29
  mini muffin 132
  mini pitta pizzas 29
  pizza toppings for baked potatoes
    140
porridge 10
potatoes
  baked 139
  toppings for 74–5, 138–40
power-packed oat bars with
  cranberries, apricots and pumpkin
  seeds 178–9
prawns
  Annabel's Pad Thai noodles 62
  Annabel's paella 76–7
  baked potato toppings with 74,
    75
  easy prawn pilau 78
  korma curry with 82
  pasta salad with 37

Index

prawn and watercress sandwiches 36

Singapore noodles 63

stir-fried rice with chicken and 105

processed foods 6, 9

protein 7–8

puddings 144–63

pumpkin seeds 178, 185

spiced pumpkin muffins 185

R

raisins 168

chewy oatmeal raisin cookies 168

oat, raisin and sunflower seed cookies 45

raspberries

honey-layered yoghurt with blueberries and 147

lemon mousse with crushed meringue and raspberries 146

raspberry ripple desert 150

red onions 130–1

red peppers 77, 99

Annabel's paella 76–7

turkey salad with sweetcorn and roast pepper 99

redcurrants, ruby fruit salad 155

rhubarb

and strawberry crumble 154

and strawberry lolly 162

rice

baked risotto with tomato, courgette and Parmesan 137

cheesy tomato rice 136

easy Chinese fried 72

easy prawn pilau 78

egg fried 89

korma curry with prawns 82

salmon kedgeree 82

sloppy Joe with 113

stir-fried rice with chicken and prawns 105

Rice Krispie squares 175–6, 182–3

rösti, vegetable 136

ruby fruit salad 155

S

salads

Chef's 37

chopped Cobb 34–5

couscous salad with turkey, cranberries and pecans 95

dark salad leaves 34

pasta and chicken salad with honey and soy vinaigrette 33

pasta salad with prawns 37

pasta shell salad with chicken and sweetcorn 32

salad kebabs 38, 39

spinach salad with mango and strawberries 134–5

tomato and mozzarella 30–1

turkey salad with sweetcorn and roast pepper 99

salmon 71

Annabel's mini fish pie 83

bow tie pasta with salmon 70

easy salmon fish cakes 78

glazed salmon with couscous 79

honey and soy salmon kebabs 71

salmon kedgeree 82

sticky 72

tasty salmon and spinach pie 84–5

salt 9

sandwiches, prawn and watercress 36

satay, chicken 93, 96–7

sesame seeds 90–1

Jacques's sesame chicken fingers 90–1

sesame beef stir fry 116

shallots 118

Singapore noodles 63

smoothies 46–7

snacks 6, 10, 16–47

soups

butternut squash, carrot and ginger 128

chicken soup with sweetcorn 88

golden lentil and vegetable 129

Thai-style chicken 88

tomato soup with pasta stars 128

spaghetti

Caroline's turkey meatballs with spaghetti and tomato sauce 66–7

with plum and sunblush tomatoes 51

primavera 142–3

spaghettini with chicken, tomatoes and basil 50

with tomato sauce 61

traditional spaghetti Bolognese 118

spiced pumpkin muffins 185

spinach

chicken teriyaki with spinach 100

cream cheese, spinach and tomato wrap 133

giant pasta shells with spinach and ricotta 54–5

salad with mango and strawberries 134–5

tasty salmon and spinach pie 84–5

spring menu planner 12

sticky salmon 72

strawberries 159

Eton mess 159

mango and strawberries with passion fruit sauce 147

rhubarb and strawberry crumble 154

spinach salad with mango and 134–5

strawberry and lychee lolly 160, 161

sugar intake 9

summer berry yoghurt ice cream 156, 157

summer menu planner 13

sweet and sour chicken 89

sweetcorn 32

Chef's salad 37

chicken satay with Chinese leaf, beansprouts and baby sweetcorn 96–7

chicken soup with 88

mini pitta pizzas 29

pasta shell salad with chicken and 32

pitta pockets stuffed with tuna, egg and 24

turkey salad with sweetcorn and roast pepper 99

T

tartare sauce, gougons of fish with 80–1

teriyaki chicken skewers 92

teriyaki steak 108
Thai-style chicken soup 88
tofu and vegetable burgers 133
tomato sauce recipes 50, 51, 59, 61, 64–5, 66–7, 141
tomatoes 61, 112
   baked risotto with tomato, courgette and Parmesan 137
   cheesy tomato rice 136
   chicken wrap with tomato pesto 19
   cream cheese, spinach and tomato wrap 133
   penne with tuna and tomato 70
   tomato and mozzarella salad 30–1
   tomato soup with pasta stars 128
tortilla wraps *see* wraps
traditional spaghetti Bolognese 118
tuna 8
   baked potato toppings 74
   melt 27
   penne with tuna and tomato 70
   pitta pockets stuffed with tuna, egg and sweetcorn 24

turkey 95
   Caroline's turkey meatballs with spaghetti and tomato sauce 66–7
   Chef's salad 37
   couscous salad with turkey, cranberries and pecans 95
   meatloaf 104
   pasta salad with honey and soy sauce dressing 52
   salad with sweetcorn and roast pepper 99

V
veal 124
   Milanese 124
vegetables, recipes 57, 64–5, 126–43, 136

W
water 8, 11
watermelon
   cocktail 46
   cooler 162

Welsh rarebit 27
white Rice Krispie squares 175–6
wholegrain cereal 169
winter menu planner 15
wraps
   caramelized red onion and mozzarella 130–1
   chicken Caesar 18
   chicken wrap with tomato pesto 19
   Chinese chicken 20–1
   cream cheese, banana and honey 22
   cream cheese, spinach and tomato 133
   Mexican egg wrap 19
   prawn and lettuce 18

Y
yoghurt 150, 161
   honey-layered yoghurt with blueberries and raspberries 147
   luscious lychee frozen yoghurt 156
   summer berry yoghurt ice cream 156, 157

Index

Show a/n
S 7|17

Acknowledgements

I want to thank my three children, Nicholas, Lara and Scarlett, for being such wonderful guinea pigs for all my new recipes and bearing with me for working long hours into the night on this book. I also want to thank all their many friends for being such willing consumer panels to my triumphs and failures. My house has become a prime destination for hungry teenagers at mealtimes…

Many thanks to Marina Magpoc, Letty Catada and Caroline Brewester for assisting me in testing the recipes for the book. Simon Karmel, who should be renamed Oliver because he always asks for more. Evelyn Etkind, my mum, for stealing the finished recipes and taking them home with her to entertain her friends.

I would like to thank Seki Tijani, who worked alongside me highlighting the nutritional benefits of each recipe, and proving that something that tastes good can also be good for you. Thanks also to Fiona Hunter for checking the accuracy of the nutritional information throughout.

I also want to thank my amazing book team: Dave King, my photographer, stylist and set designer all rolled into one, and Dagmar Vesely, who makes my recipes look so mouth-watering. Sarah Lavelle, Carey Smith, Helena Caldon, Lisa Pettibone and Fiona MacIntyre at Ebury Press, who put up with my quest for perfection.

A big thank you to Jacqui Morley, Mary Jones and David Karmel, who help bring some organization into my chaotic life, and Jacques Tredoux for the almost impossible task of harnessing my energy in the right direction.

A big thank you to all the gorgeous children who modelled for the book: Olivia Cantalon, Sean Ekon, Brian, Alex and Isabelle Hnat, Scarlett Karmel, Max Menaged, Nicola and Jessica Tredoux.

I hope this book will have your children rushing back from school with their friends in anticipation of the tasty meals and treats you will soon have in store for them…

About the author

'Any mother who does not have at least one of Annabel's books in her kitchen, well thumbed and splattered with food, should waste no time in putting that right.' *The Sunday Times*

Annabel is the author of 14 best-selling books focusing on nutrition and cooking for babies, toddlers and families. She is the leading expert on creating healthy food that children like to eat and tasty family meals that don't require parents to spend hours in the kitchen.

The mother of three children, Annabel was inspired to write children's cookery books following the death of her first child Natasha, who died of a rare viral disease aged just three months. Although the illness was not diet-related, it strengthened Annabel's belief that what your child eats determines his or her future health. Having lost a child, Annabel was determined to give her second child the best possible start in life; he turned out to be an incredibly fussy eater, and she spent two years researching child nutrition and development, interviewing leading paediatricians and nutritionists and working with Great Ormond Street Hospital for Children.

Published in 1991, Annabel's first book, *The Complete Baby and Toddler Meal Planner*, has become the definitive guide on feeding babies and toddlers and is now sold all over the world. Total sales are now several million and it remains steadily in the top five best-selling cookery books

in the UK. Annabel has since produced a further 13 books, ranging from *Superfoods for Babies and Children*, *Top 100 Baby Purées* to *Lunchboxes* and *Favourite Family Recipes*.

Annabel is the expert in getting your child, no matter how fussy, to eat a healthier diet – without them even noticing! She has developed tricks to improve your children's diet, from hiding vegetables in other foods, packing powerhouse lunchboxes and creating healthy junk food to showing parents the superfoods kids should be eating to boost brainpower!

Annabel writes regularly for national newspapers including *The Times*, *Mail* and *Sunday Mirror* and also writes for *Practical Parenting*, *BBC Good Food Magazine* and *Sainsbury's Magazine*. She appears frequently on radio and television as the UK's expert on children's nutritional issues. Recently, she completed a series on Channel 4's *Richard and Judy Show* as the 'Foodie Godmother', where she travelled around England helping to solve the eating problems of ultra-fussy eaters. Annabel's books are published all over the world and she travels frequently to the United States. Annabel is a celebrity chef on the BBC website. She also has her own website: www.annabelkarmel.com which offers lots of recipes and advice.

Annabel has recently launched an extensive range of cooking equipment and foods to help parents prepare their own fresh baby and toddler food, called 'Make Your Own'.

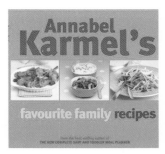
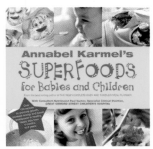